Gertrude J. Coward

Sept. 8, 1992

TERRA-COTTA SOLDIERS AND HORSES IN PIT NO. 1, LINTONG, XI'AN, CHINA

MYSTERIES OF MANKIND

Earth's Unexplained Landmarks

Prepared by the Book Division
National Geographic Society, Washington, D. C.

STONEHENGE, ENGLAND; HALLEY'S COMET OVER EASTER ISLAND, CHILE (PRECEDING PAGES)

MYSTERIES OF MANKIND
Earth's Unexplained Landmarks

Contributing Authors: Anthony F. Aveni,
  Brian M. Fagan, Ann Nottingham Kelsall,
  Tom Melham, Cynthia Russ Ramsay,
  Gene S. Stuart, George E. Stuart,
  Jo Anne Van Tilburg
Contributing Photographer: James A. Sugar
Paintings by H. Tom Hall

Published by The National Geographic Society
Gilbert M. Grosvenor,
  President and Chairman of the Board
Michela A. English, *Senior Vice President*

Prepared by The Book Division

William R. Gray, *Vice President and Director*
Margery G. Dunn, Charles Kogod,
  Assistant Directors

Staff for this book

Mary B. Dickinson, Gene S. Stuart,
  Managing Editors
Greta Arnold, *Illustrations Editor*
Jody Bolt, *Art Director*
Victoria Cooper, *Senior Researcher*
Melanie Patt-Corner, Penelope A. Timbers,
  Researchers
Richard M. Crum, Ann Nottingham Kelsall,
  Tom Melham, Cynthia Russ Ramsay,

Gene S. Stuart, George E. Stuart,
Jennifer C. Urquhart, *Picture Legend Writers*

Gary M. Johnson, Daniel J. Ortiz,
Map Research and Production

Sandra F. Lotterman, *Editorial Assistant*

Artemis S. Lampathakis,
Illustrations Assistant

Lewis R. Bassford,
Production Project Manager

Heather Guwang, H. Robert Morrison,
Richard S. Wain, *Production*

Karen F. Edwards, Elizabeth G. Jevons,
Teresita Cóquia Sison, Karen Dufort Sligh,
Marilyn J. Williams, *Staff Assistants*

Manufacturing and Quality Management

George V. White, *Director*
John T. Dunn, *Associate Director*
Vincent P. Ryan, *Manager*
and R. Gary Colbert

Bryan K. Knedler, *Indexer*

Library of Congress ᴄɪᴘ Data: page 200

TEMPLE OF THE FOLIATED CROSS, PALENQUE, MEXICO

Prologue:
Giza and Knossos

THE LURE OF MYSTERIES

by George E. Stuart

"We know only too well that all over the world . . . there are people, otherwise sensible and sane, people who would not believe in six-headed cats and blood-curdling spectral monsters, who yet read some folly about Noah's ark or Atlantis or cataclysmic world-tides, and say, with a contented sigh, 'There may be something in it, you know.' "

Glyn Daniel, archaeologist

People are intrigued by a mystery, and the Aztecs of Mexico were no exception. Unable to account for the huge and enigmatic ruined city that lay near their bustling capital, they ascribed it to supernatural builders – and named it Teotihuacan, "place of the gods." Some things have changed very little in the past 700 or so years, for I recently read that ancient astronauts built Teotihuacan. I have also read that refugees from the lost continent of Atlantis were the ancestors of the American Indians.

On the other hand, my archaeologist colleagues contend that Mexican Indians built Teotihuacan and thrived in the ancient metropolis through the first seven centuries of the Christian era. They think that ancestors of the American Indians came from Asia beginning at least 15,000 years ago. What, then, should one believe? Sometimes that question seems to me fully as difficult for us as it must have been for the Aztecs.

By definition, archaeologists deal with mysteries, and the number of unanswered questions about the ancient world is infinite. Who made the Nazca lines in southern Peru, or built Stonehenge, and why? With the help of physicists, linguists, art historians, and other specialists, archaeologists have

Mystery manifest in stone, the Sphinx at Giza has awed the curious for some 4,500 years. Archaeologists believe it memorializes the Pharaoh Khafre, builder of one of the nearby pyramids.

PRECEDING PAGES: Panorama of Giza's three pyramids, built between about 2800 and 2400 B.C., dwarfs the Sphinx, lower right, and sprawling tombs of the city of the dead.

RICHARD STEEDMAN / THE STOCK MARKET; TOR EIGELAND (PRECEDING PAGES)

attacked such mysteries for more than a century. We have often succeeded not only in reconstructing the chronology of prehistoric events but also in explaining puzzling details. Archaeologists, however, are not alone in confronting the mysteries of the past, for another, drastically different approach exists in which there are no rules. My colleague Stephen Williams of Harvard University calls it "fantastic archaeology."

Fantastic archaeology, as Steve defines it, is false "science" that has flourished alongside scientific archaeology. The fantastic archaeologists and their followers see no mystery as unsolvable, no question unanswerable, and no ancient script undecipherable. We see signs of fantastic archaeology in the headlines of supermarket tabloids ("Mummy of Alien Found in Arizona") and in books that conjure up everything from ancient astronauts to superficial similarities in art or language as "evidence" of ancient migrations or of past achievement.

For me, the most damaging of the beliefs endorsed by the fantastic archaeologists is the implicit assumption that every culture that existed before their own time was composed of stumbling blockheads. Perhaps the best example of this kind of solution to mysteries of the past is proposed by Erich von Däniken in his *Chariots of the Gods?*, which credits everything from the Nazca lines to the sculptures of Easter Island to extraterrestrials who came to earth thousands of years ago and gave its presumably doltish inhabitants the gift of high civilization.

The differences between scientific archaeology and fantastic archaeology are perhaps most evident in Egypt. About a hundred pyramids of various sizes dot the landscape along the Nile, some alone, others in clusters. Those at Giza, across the river from Cairo, include the largest one of all. The Great Pyramid contains an estimated 2.3 million building stones carefully placed in a stupendous pile of symmetry. Nearby lie two smaller pyramids, the famed Sphinx, and a complicated array of other remains. The Great Pyramid holds several interior passageways, and the main one reaches a chamber at the center. In it lies an empty sarcophagus of rose-colored granite.

Archaeologists say that the coffin once held the remains of Khufu, or Cheops, who ruled Egypt between 2789 and 2767 B.C. Evidence gathered by scientific archaeologists through excavation and the dating of artifacts, coupled with hieroglyphic texts at Giza, points to the conclusion that the Great Pyramid is the gigantic tomb of a man of awesome power and stands as one of the world's greatest monuments of human engineering and architecture.

Enter the fantastic archaeologists. In 1859 the eccentric John Taylor of London began the pseudoscience of "pyramidology" with a book on the Great Pyramid (which he never visited). Taylor perceived the structure as divinely directed and speculated that Noah built it soon after the biblical deluge. From the dimensions of the pyramid – and he depended on drawings of varying accuracy – Taylor derived a plethora of mathematical coincidences, including a "sacred cubit" based on the length of the earth's axis.

Between 1864 and 1867, Piazzi Smyth, the Astronomer Royal of Scotland, carried Taylor's work further in *Our Inheritance in the Great Pyramid.* Smyth "refined" the proposed sacred cubit and produced another unit of

Majorville
▲ ▲Moose
  ▲ Mountain
Bighorn

Stonehenge ▲

Knossos
▲
Giza ▲

Mount Li ▲

Pacific
Ocean

Atlantic
Ocean

Palenque ▲

Pacific
Ocean

Nan ▲
Madol

Indian
Ocean

Nazca ▲

Great ▲
Zimbabwe ▲

▲ Easter
  Island

*Mysteries of the earth's human past —
and many answers as well — are
revealed by remains left in every
habitable area of the planet. Those
described in this book, at the sites
indicated above, span more than 50
centuries of cultural history.*

measure, the "pyramid inch." Smyth spent four months measuring the Great Pyramid. By combining his numbers in arbitrary ways, he derived, among other things, the distance from the earth to the sun. And by equating one pyramid inch to a 365-day year, Smyth reconstructed his version of the history and future of the earth by intervals he perceived in the stone passageways. Other fantastic archaeologists have manipulated the Great Pyramid and concluded, with the same zealous sincerity, that the imposing structure functioned as an observatory, a granary, or a gigantic hydraulic apparatus that pumped water from the Nile.

Across the Mediterranean from Egypt lie the ruins of Knossos, Bronze Age capital of Crete, and its complex building known as the Labyrinth or the Palace of Minos. Like the Great Pyramid, the palace poses many mysteries, and for nearly a century archaeologists have taken them on. Sir Arthur Evans, who excavated the structure over the first quarter of this century, concluded that the building was the dwelling of the legendary King Minos. He also believed it to be the site of the fabled Labyrinth where Theseus and his lover Ariadne, daughter of King Minos, tracked and killed the Minotaur, the hideous man-bull monster.

In his interpretation of the structure, Evans may have relied too heavily on ambiguous clues in the works of Homer, Plutarch, Herodotus, and other classical historians and poets. In other words, it makes a fine story, but is it true? Recently archaeologists have begun to question some of Evans's deductions, based on a more complete knowledge of the eastern Mediterranean during the second millennium B.C. and on clues in his meticulous excavation notes. They conclude that the palace functioned much like a medieval European abbey, as both temple and market. It contained storerooms for the redistribution of livestock, grain, wine, and other Cretan products, while chambers in a nearby building appear to have served as grim sanctuaries for secret cults of child sacrifice and ritual cannibalism. Did King Minos even exist? Probably — or perhaps many rulers bore the name. Did he, or they, live in the "palace"? Probably not, according to new studies. Besides, a yet unexcavated structure nearby makes a more logical candidate.

Recalling my own impression of the building as reconstructed by Evans, I can only agree with the writer who called the palace "one of the great tourist-befuddlers of the ages." Obviously, it is also a befuddler of archaeologists. But at least the scientific investigator of Knossos possesses evidence that is both well documented and testable. Thus the real story of Knossos awaits the telling — and I am sure that it, too, will be a good one.

Scientific archaeology at both Giza and Knossos shows us that the most wondrous monuments of the past are the products of humans whose talents rose to all occasions, no matter the time, the place, or the culture. In other words, solutions to our mysteries do not lie in fantasy or convenient inventions that defy scientific evaluation, such as extraterrestrials or the mythical continents of Atlantis and Mu. It's not that archaeologists oppose ancient astronauts or sunken civilizations as such, only that they have committed themselves to carefully following the evidence to the best of their ability, and to this day there has been no proof that either speculation is true.

It would be an act of monumental arrogance to believe that today we know everything about those who lived before. Or that the things we do know are correct, for we have seen how the interpretations of scientific archaeology can change. Indeed, we have at hand enough mysteries about the past to keep scientists busy until the end of time. At Giza, for example, remains of what appears to be the village of the workers who built the Great Pyramid have begun to come to light. This excavation will doubtless give us fresh answers about the place and its people — and create questions we haven't even thought of yet. Ironically, Piazzi Smyth's book about the Great Pyramid has been reprinted just in time to perpetuate the confusion!

This book presents a selection of ancient mysteries that span the world. Each has fascinated people for centuries, and most have at one time or another been the target of both fantastic archaeology and scientific archaeology. And, as you will see, each has also yielded answers that more often than not prove even more incredible than fantasies.

Newly discovered burial chambers at Giza once held the remains of Egyptians of rank. Here, some 4,000 members of royal households of the third millennium B.C. were buried.

FOLLOWING PAGES: A marvel of ancient engineering skill, the Great Pyramid contains some 2.3 million blocks of stone, many quarried across the Nile, miles away from the site.

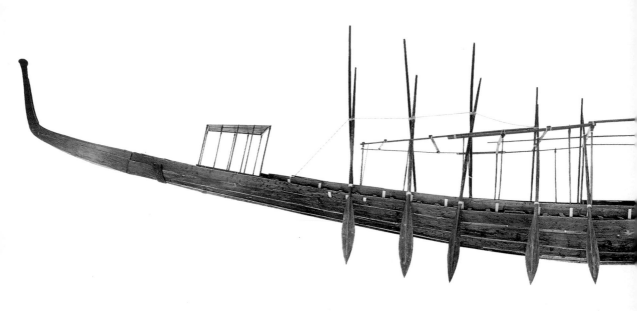

*E*ternal waters of the Nile formed
the fragile thread of life for ancient
Egypt and became part of its rich
fabric of religion and cosmology.
Papyrus from the river marshes (left)
gave its name to paper. It helped
Egyptians to maintain records of their
lives and beliefs. Funerary boats such
as the one above, found dismantled
in a special pit near the base of the
Great Pyramid, matched those that
cruised the Nile. Such boats,
Egyptians believed, served to carry
the dead pharaoh into the afterworld.

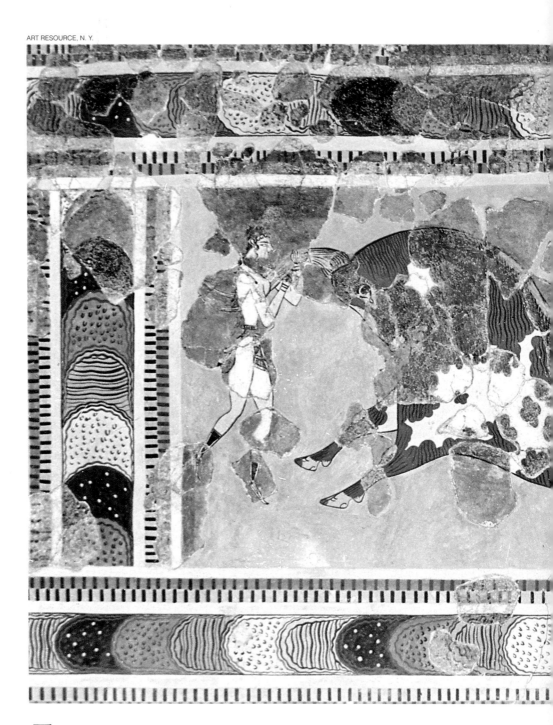

Frozen at the crucial stage of a dangerous game, two agile girls and a boy defy a fearsome charging bull in a mural of the second millennium B.C., *miraculously preserved at Knossos. Bull-leaping, depicted also on rings, vases, and other objects, demanded a carefully timed somersault over a charging bull. The potentially lethal pastime remains*

*mysterious to modern experts, who
disagree about its purpose. Some see
it as simply a dangerous and
enthralling sport, perhaps performed
on special religious occasions.*

The greatest myth of ancient Knossos, the defeat of the dread Minotaur by the hero Theseus, comes to life on a painted vase (below) of the sixth century B.C. Ruins at Knossos (opposite) feature sunken chambers perhaps used for ritual cleansing.

FOLLOWING PAGES: Remains of a 3,000-year-old sanctuary or royal villa rise from the residential zone surrounding the palace at Knossos. Largely unexcavated, the area promises to reveal details about lives spent in the shadow of the palace.

Palenque

MESSAGES TO THE GODS

by Gene S. Stuart

In the waning light at sunset, as I walk trails that lead past Palenque's ghostly structures, a ritual begins. The dead city stirs with sounds of unseen life. In a moment preordained by nature, the harmonious hum of mosquitoes and other small insects starts, then soars, falls, rises again. A shrill chorus of frogs and the melodious calls of birds join in. And from somewhere in the darkening canopy of tropical trees come the unnerving jaguar-roars of howler monkeys.

I have walked these trails many times in different seasons. I have joined scholars to explore the site in winter, when we donned gloves and hugged woolen wraps close in the unseasonable cold. Our words took on vaporous shapes in the crisp air, as if they were glyphs suspended near our mouths like those in ancient Maya carvings. I have visited the ruins in summer with my family, when oppressive noonday heat has palpable weight, when lightning explodes from sudden rainy season storms, scenting the air with its power, and thunder reverberates through a sheltering stone temple. The first giant raindrops clatter against masses of tropical leaves, then the downpour increases until, in full force, the storm veils other buildings with billowing curtains of rain.

Palenque nestles in a lap of landscape where steep mountains, lush with rain forest, meet low hills that give onto grassy plains and vast swamplands. There, in the Mexican state of Chiapas, a network of streams stretches north from the mountains toward the Gulf of Mexico, some 80 miles away.

The city probably began its rise in the fourth century A.D.; at some time in the early ninth century it was mysteriously abandoned. Its peak of grandeur came late in the Maya Classic Period, from A.D. 650 to 750. Palenque

Howler monkeys of the rain forest appeared in Maya art as scribes with ink pots and brushes. Often depicted as twin deities, they patronized writing, artists, and calculations.

PRECEDING PAGES: Raised to the glory of gods and kings, the towered Palace and the terraced Temple of the Inscriptions stand at the heart of the great Maya city-state of Palenque.

flourished when great Maya lords ruled city-states in present-day southeastern Mexico and Central America. Art historian Merle Greene Robertson writes: "If one city can be spoken of as the most exquisite, the 'jewel of the Maya realm,' it is Palenque."

For more than a thousand years this city-state lay forgotten by the outside world. But some Maya remembered the ancients. Working in Guatemala late in the 19th century, archaeologist Teobert Maler wrote, "The Mayas believe that at midnight . . . their ancestors return to earth and, adorned as in the days of their glory, wander about in the forsaken temples and palaces, where their spirit voices are heard in the air." The Maya of Mexico's Lacandon forest made pilgrimages to Palenque from time to time, slipping into the jungle-clad ruins to gaze upon the temples and the ancient stone and stucco figures and to marvel at the enigmatic glyphs. There they chanted prayers, made offerings of food, and burned incense. They had not forgotten: Palenque was a city of the gods.

Around 1750, when Chiapas was still part of the Spanish colony of Guatemala, news of this puzzling place (then called Casas de Piedras, "stone houses") began to spread beyond the mountains. Antonio del Río, an artillery captain, led an exploration of the site in May 1787. On the first day he encountered "a fog so extremely dense, that it was impossible to distinguish each other at the distance of five paces; and whereby the principal building, surrounded by copse wood and trees of large dimensions, in full foliage and closely interwoven, was completely concealed from our view."

Del Río ordered the site to be cleared. Overwhelmed by what he saw, he surmised that "the Phoenicians, the Greeks, the Romans. . . . some one of these nations pursued their conquests even to this country. . . ." He observed wistfully that the inhabitants must have enjoyed a better life "than all the concentrated luxury and refinement of the most polished cities at the present period can produce."

Local Maya probably first called del Río's "principal building" the Palace, and they were right to do so. It sprawls in the center of the city—a complex of apartments, courtyards, galleries, and a unique four-storied tower—and probably served as both royal residence and administrative hub.

Nearby, rising from the base of a steep hillside and echoing its shape, looms an equally well-known structure, a pyramid of nine terraces topped by the Temple of the Inscriptions, so called because its interior walls bear panels inscribed with glyphs—620 of them. They are exquisitely carved in low relief on dense, fine-grained limestone. One of the treasures of the ancient art world, they form the longest intact Maya text yet discovered.

What do these symbols mean? Who built the city and carved them? Why? These questions have lured adventurers and scholars to Palenque ever since its discovery.

Del Río and other 18th-century travelers saw correlations in biblical and classical lore. In the 19th century a host of explorers and gentlemen-eccentrics came from Europe, but it was American travel writer John Lloyd Stephens and English artist Frederick Catherwood who, after visiting the site in 1840, provided enlightened explanations for Palenque.

Stephens wrote of the Palace: "For the first time we were in a building erected by the aboriginal inhabitants. It had been standing there before the Europeans knew of the existence of this continent, and we prepared to take up our abode under its roof." He set up camp, feeling "admiration and astonishment" at the end of his first day in Palenque.

Stephens knew he would be lost in the treacherous ruins without a guide. He hired a man who had assisted other visitors and would have been hard to lose even in difficult terrain. One writer described him as "dressed in a sort of uniform with a pair of fringe epauletts and overalls of tanned leather with innumerable little buttons down the sides, and his horse was caparisoned in black leather trappings that gave it the appearance of a Rhinoceros."

When Stephens scrambled up the ruined pyramid now known as the Temple of the Inscriptions, he found wall panels with "complicated, unintelligible, and anomalous characters." Catherwood set about drawing these glyphs. Stephens wondered as to their meaning. "The Indians call this building an *escuela*, or school, but our friends, the padres, called it a tribunal of justice, and these stones, they said, contained the tables of the law."

Many 19th-century antiquarians fantasized about Maya history. One French cleric, on studying some Maya glyphs, believed he found in them an *M* and a *U*. He claimed a discovery of great significance—Mu, a lost continent in the Pacific. An archaeologist then read in the glyphs about Mu's cataclysmic demise and the flight of some of its inhabitants to Central America where, as the Maya, they built cities and wrote the history of Mu.

Others of that time, however, laid the foundation for modern Maya studies. By the end of the 19th century a few scholars had made an amazing discovery: Some Maya glyphs are dates. The 20th century brought increased expertise in the fields of anthropology, archaeology, art history, and linguistics. And a mid-century discovery at Palenque astonished the world.

In 1949, as Mexican archaeologist Alberto Ruz Lhuillier worked in the Temple of the Inscriptions, he examined something unusual. One of the flagstones that paved the temple floor looked different from the others: Stone plugs filled holes drilled along two of its edges. Ruz and his crew began to excavate the floor around this flagstone. Beneath it they found a vaulted stone stairway intentionally filled with rubble. It led downward into the unknown.

At that time archaeologists believed that Maya pyramids were only massive bases for the temples they supported. Ruz and his crew, puzzled by their discovery, began the painstaking labor of clearing the stairway and carefully recording the process. They removed rocks—tons of them. Ruz wrote: "The farther we descended the more difficult the work became. The rocks were raised one by one with ropes and pulleys, the dirt pail by pail; we had only one gasoline lamp that consumed much of the little oxygen that reached the bottom through the small opening in the floor of the temple. In the first season of work we uncovered twenty-three steps. . . ." A square stone tube lay attached to one wall and followed the stairs in a serpentine path.

The next season the workers changed over to electric lighting. Inching downward, they came to a landing. They were now approximately in the center of the pyramid. To their amazement, the stairway turned and led deeper.

It was not until two digging seasons later, in 1952, that Ruz reached the bottom of the stairs, 75 feet beneath the temple floor. He found two offerings – a stone box holding jade, shells, and a pearl, and an enclosure containing the bones of six young people who had been sacrificed.

Ruz had come to think that the stairs were part of a secret passage. But near the human offering he found a doorway blocked by a great triangular stone slab. He removed some stone and plaster rubble along one edge, "and through this open space I could see with the help of an electric flashlight. . . . a spacious chamber with stucco reliefs on the walls and an enormous sculpted monument that almost filled it totally." Two days later Ruz removed the great slab and entered a place kept secret for nearly 1,300 years.

Offerings of jade, mother-of-pearl, and a seashell lay on top of the huge monument, or altar, as Ruz called it. On the floor sat clay plates and vases and "two beautiful human heads modeled in stucco."

Ruz decided that the secret room was a place where priests celebrated religious ceremonies. He wondered why it had been concealed, and concluded that the "great Maya city must have been threatened by hostile invasion. . . . at the time of greatest peril, this threat induced the priests to close the secret chamber so that it might not suffer foreign profanation."

It was not until five months later that Ruz found the supposed altar was hollow. He ordered a tree felled and its trunk cut into sections. Using these and heavy jacks, the crew began to lift the top stone "millimeter by millimeter. . . . When there was sufficient room . . . I could see that the contents was a burial. For that matter, the entire chamber was a monumental sepulcher."

With the top finally removed, Ruz gazed upon "the bones of an individual who had been buried with his jewelry in place and wrapped in a red shroud. . . ." A jade mosaic mask had covered his face. Among his ornaments, all made of jade, were bracelets, a breastplate, necklaces, ear plugs, and a ring for each finger. A jade bead had been placed in his mouth.

A physical anthropologist concluded that the bones were those of a man about six feet tall who had died in his late 30s to mid-40s. Knowing that rulers in other Mexican cultures often had dates as names, Ruz believed glyphs indicated this man's name was a Maya date – 8 Ahau.

At a beach picnic in Yucatan in 1958, Alberto Ruz quietly discussed his find with me. "After all that work, all those years, I thought at first that our search led only to a solid wall – part of the pyramid construction – at the end of the corridor," he said. "I did not see the large stone concealing the doorway until later." Many scholars say Ruz's discovery was one of the greatest in 20th-century Maya archaeology.

I visited Palenque for the first time in the summer of 1965, traveling there from the Yucatan Peninsula. A paved highway did not yet link the peninsula to the rest of Mexico, so I went by train, getting off at the hot, dusty village of Palenque, whose name archaeologists had given to the ancient city. The ruins lie about five miles away. At that time, the site had fewer visitors than now. Only three people toured with me, and we climbed the steep stairs of the famous Temple of the Inscriptions, eager to visit the tomb.

To descend the interior stairway, you must cross a narrow stone slab with a sheer drop into the stairwell on one side and a wall on the other. Those more confident than I stride the few steps across it. I always turn away from the terrifying drop, face the wall, and inch along, wishing for finger holds to appear. The steep stairs, often slick with dripping moisture, tracked-in mud, and even algae, must be negotiated with caution. On that first visit, once at the bottom, I walked into the chamber and entered a fantasy world.

There, in the hot, humid tropics, a dim light illuminated a scene that seemed to be carved from ice. Nine stucco figures stood or sat along the walls and glistened as if with frost. Details had softened, some melting away, some slipping downward in a thaw of time and moisture. Snowy calcite had precipitated from the limestone and streaked the walls. In places these encrustations extended into long, thin stalactite icicles.

In the 13-by-30-foot crypt lay the sarcophagus, carved from creamy, smooth limestone. Sculptured figures around its sides seemed to rise from plants and turn to each other, gesturing in animated conversation. Carved on the top was a half-reclining person surrounded by puzzling glyphs and icons.

Through intensified research, the story of the tomb and its occupant now starts to unfold. Scholars who gathered at Palenque in December nearly two decades ago — especially linguist Floyd Lounsbury, archaeologist Peter Mathews, and art historian Linda Schele — studied glyphs in the crypt, in the temple, and in other structures. Within days, building upon earlier work and deciphering new glyphs, they made astonishing discoveries.

Glyphs revealed that the Temple of the Inscriptions entombed a man named — at least in part — Pacal, or Shield. The ten figures depicted with fruit trees on the sarcophagus sides are his royal ancestors. Pacal's mother, Lady Zac-Kuk, ruled immediately before him. Her consort, Pacal's father, was doubtless of royal lineage, but probably from another Maya city. The inscriptions combine fact with myth, tracing Lady Zac-Kuk's ancestry back to a Palenque goddess who was born around 3000 B.C. The proclamation established that she and her son, Pacal, were divine, as most Maya rulers claimed to be. Other inscriptions record that Pacal was born in March, A.D. 603, and became ruler of Palenque in July 615, when he was 12 years old. He reigned for 68 years until his death in August 683, at the age of 80.

During Pacal's long tenure, and that of his son and successor, Chan-Bahlum, the city reached its peak of magnificence. The two rulers sponsored a flowering of scholarship and skill; astronomers, mathematicians, sculptors, and architects turned the city into a great intellectual and artistic center.

Merle Greene Robertson has spent decades studying the art and architecture of Palenque, a city she calls "an epic poem scribed in stone and stucco." The work of Merle and other scholars has also brought to light the Maya worldview and revealed beliefs essential for understanding the tomb.

The Maya believed that time revolved in recurring cycles, with propitious dates and days to be dreaded. Above earth stretched the layers of heaven. A gigantic, sacred ceiba tree connected earth with these realms of the gods. Beneath the earth lay the dark, fearsome underworld, into which the sun set and traveled through the night to rise again triumphant at dawn. The elite dead also made this treacherous journey before rising to join their celestial ancestors. Mountains were sacred, and caves were entries to the underworld. Architecture held symbolic meaning. The Maya built pyramids to represent mountains; temple doorways were like the mouths of caves. World trees rose from temples; a city of many temples was a sacred forest.

As Pacal grew old, he planned his funeral monument at a spot near the Palace. In their book *The Blood of Kings*, art historians Mary Ellen Miller and Linda Schele explain: "The king sited the Temple of Inscriptions along the line connecting the center of the palace with one of the most important alignments of the sun in the tropical year. At the winter solstice, the sun reaches its southernmost point, setting exactly on the line that runs through the tomb."

Pacal ordered that his sarcophagus would show him surrounded by ancestors, representing a royal orchard bearing fruit. On the lid, the king slips in death down the world tree toward the maw of the underworld. He is like a setting sun; he sits on the head of the sun god, who is ready to disappear below the horizon. The stucco figures on the walls are gods.

Solutions, however, have created new mysteries. Was Pacal indeed 80 when he died? Would a reexamination of his bones using the latest technology confirm or disprove that he died at a younger age? Some scholars suggest that he did live to be 80, then selected a date and had himself sacrificed. Parts of the sarcophagus still bear painted black lines indicating where sculptors should carve. Why was it left unfinished and the temple constructed over it? And what was the purpose of the stone tube that archaeologists call a psychoduct? Many scholars believe it provided a way for the dead king to communicate with the living.

Had Pacal and his great dynasty been forgotten? Perhaps not. A Lacandon Maya chief, Chan K'in (Little Sun) said that lords were buried beneath buildings at Palenque long before he heard of Ruz's discovery.

Just as in the 18th and 19th centuries, some people still offer explanations of the tomb based only on their own knowledge. During the heat of space-age excitement, one popular theory saw ancient astronauts from another planet visiting earth and constructing Maya cities. The sarcophagus lid showed Pacal reclining in a rocket seat and preparing to blast off. More recently, a civil engineer proposed that the scene shows Pacal with one foot poised to press a pedal in a gigantic earth-moving machine.

On my last visit to Palenque, I descended into the tomb with Merle Robertson. An iron grille now keeps the traffic of visitors outside the crypt, but we entered so that she could check her drawings of the sarcophagus. Ancestors, gods, the world tree — now I understood that the chamber was filled with Pacal's identity and his messages to the gods. We knelt to examine the ancestral orchard. As Merle worked, I rose slowly until the lid was at my eye level.

It was then that I noticed. Wind, rain, and constant visitors had brought the living world of nature into this entry to the underworld. In the darkness, tiny seeds had sprouted. Their tender stems and leaves bore the tentative pastel colors of new life — beige, pink, the palest of greens. From the carved crevices of the world tree and the king there grew a forest in miniature.

Stucco sculpture likely portrays Pacal at 12, when his 68-year rule began in A.D. 615. Under his leadership, Palenque grew into a major city — and a center for learning and the arts.

FOLLOWING PAGES: Still lovingly maintained by the living, the Temple of the Inscriptions honored the dead. Interior glyphs record history. Piers bear sculptures of kings and gods.

JEAN-PIERRE COURAU / EXPLORER; ANDREAS STERZING (FOLLOWING PAGES)

*S*tairway into the unknown, discovered in 1949, led archaeologists to a forgotten crypt 80 feet beneath the temple. A square stone tube, tracing one edge of the stairs, may have allowed the spirit of Pacal to contact the living. Carvings on the 5-ton sarcophagus lid symbolize his death, his journey through the Maya cosmos, and his rebirth as a deity.

FOLLOWING PAGES: Morning mist enshrouds the heart of Palenque. The Temple of the Count, in the foreground, was named for the Comte de Waldeck, who explored the ruins in the 1830s. Scholars believe construction of the Temple of the Inscriptions, at right in the background, took 15 years as it rose above the crypt and sarcophagus.

*P*alace gallery shows the ravages of time — and vestiges of splendor. On a stone tablet, Lady Zac-Kuk presents the royal headdress of Palenque to her son, the youthful Pacal, during his enthronement in A.D. 615. The Palace served as a governing center and a mystical setting for elite rituals.

T-shaped opening in the form of the glyph *ik* adorns a Palace wall. Palenque architecture often included this puzzling symbol. The name of a day in the Maya month, *ik* means wind, soul, or spirit. *Ik* openings may have been used as sighting devices or as ventilators.

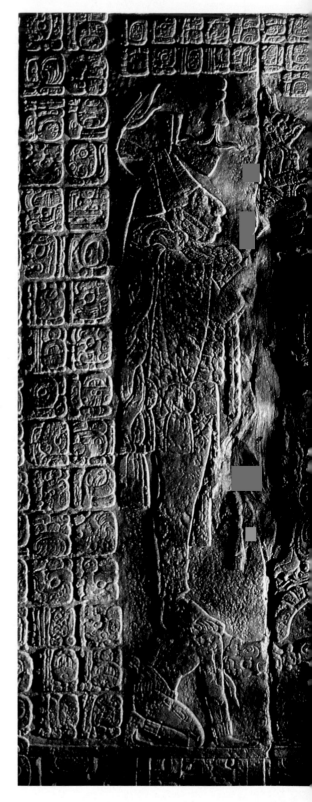

*M*aya writing (above) expresses a lordly title at top left. Three glyph syllables on the right spell out a king's name: pa-ca-la — Pacal. In the Temple of the Sun Tablet (right), Pacal's son Chan-Bahlum is designated royal heir as a boy, then, as an adult, accepts the office of king. The figures flank the Jaguar God shield, and glyphs trace royal lineage and divinity. Pacal and Chan-Bahlum's combined 87-year regime saw Palenque reach its peak of sophistication and power.

FOLLOWING PAGES: From the Palace roof spreads a view of ruined Temple XIV and Chan-Bahlum's three memorial structures, the Cross Group, including, at right, the Temple of the Sun. Panels in his temples record Chan-Bahlum's ancestry and events of his reign from A.D. 684 to 702.

Mount Li

WHERE THE TIGER HOLDS COURT

by Ann Nottingham Kelsall

"U.S. Flier Reports Huge Chinese Pyramid In Isolated Mountains Southwest of Sian," read a *New York Times* headline on March 28, 1947. This was not the first time Col. Maurice Sheahan had seen the great mound in China's Shaanxi Province. He had spotted it from an airplane while working for the Chinese government before the Second World War. During the war he served as a U.S. Army officer and for a time as supply officer to the fabled Flying Tigers. Now, after the war's end, he had returned to take a closer look.

The colonel described the location as being 40 miles southwest of Sian, the provincial capital, now spelled Xi'an. From the air he estimated the pyramid's height to be 1,000 feet and its width at the base 1,500 feet. At that size it would dwarf even the Great Pyramid of Giza in Egypt.

A flurry of reports and speculations followed in the American press. A scholarly commentary described the find as being "like the discovery of a new planet whose existence had been anticipated even though it had never been seen. . . ." The *American Weekly* embellished the initial report, insisting that there were actually two huge pyramids, not one, and that they might be as much as 4,000 years old.

Professor Derk Bodde, a China specialist at the University of Pennsylvania, was quoted in the *Philadelphia Inquirer* as saying that the pyramid probably was the tomb of China's First Emperor, and if so, dated from the Qin dynasty in the third century B.C. Local Chinese officials added to the general confusion by dismissing the reports altogether. On March 31 representatives of the Xi'an government announced that they had investigated Colonel Sheahan's claims, and the giant pyramid did not exist.

Stories about the Great Wall form part of the myth surrounding China's First Emperor. He marshaled a huge work force to build frontier ramparts, but few Qin dynasty sections survive.

PRECEDING PAGES: Ranks scattered in disorder, excavated terra-cotta images of the First Emperor's elite infantrymen stand guard on the outer perimeter of his tomb site near Xi'an.

Both Professor Bodde and the Chinese officials were correct. The tumulus that Colonel Sheahan saw from the air was indeed the Qin tomb, the burial place of China's First Emperor, but the colonel's estimates of its height were exceedingly generous, and his estimates of the location were off by some 50 miles. Even though Xi'an is one of China's ancient imperial capital cities, and monumental tombs are almost commonplace in the nearby countryside, there are none of note in the rugged mountains to the southwest.

The colonel's pyramid was not where he said it was, nor was he the first Westerner to discover it. The great tumulus was already known to Western sinologists by at least the 1920s, and an American guidebook described it and located it correctly in Lintong County. A French archaeological report published in 1924 provided photographic evidence. To most Westerners, however, China had long been a mysterious place, primarily of interest to missionaries and archaeologists, until war bound us together as allies. After the war, curiosity was great, and there was much to discover. But for the Chinese, one fearful struggle had just ended and another, a costly civil war, was about to begin. Speculation as to the contents or the meaning of the tomb of a discredited emperor was a luxury they were not ready to afford.

Today a highway connects Xi'an with the flat, dusty reaches of the narrow Wei River Valley. The road skirts the graceful ridges of Mount Li just to the south and the banks of the Wei River to the north. Peasant farmers, pulling, pushing, or riding in their wobbly carts, compete for road room with caravans of dilapidated, sputtering local buses, fleets of sleek coaches from distant cities, and brightly colored vans emblazoned with the logos of luxury hotels. The air holds the churning dust suspended, releasing it like drizzle onto the surface of anything that passes through. A cacophony of automobile horns mixes with the jangle of bells, shouts, whistles, and choruses of peddlers waving their goods to the chant of "Cheap, cheap, cheap."

I revisited Lintong County in the autumn of 1990 with Zhu Jian, a graduate student at Jiaotong University where I was teaching English. He had come to Shaanxi Province only recently, and this was his first visit to Mount Li. The day was beautiful, and we had throngs of company, most of them Chinese. It was too late in the season for most Western tourists.

Rattling along in the crush of traffic, the first-time traveler on this stretch of highway can easily bounce past the tumulus without seeing it. The great mound is so large and rises so gracefully against the shadow of the nearby hills that it seems an act of nature. Only its nearly perfect symmetry betrays it as man-made. We left our university car and driver—assigned to us for the day—and climbed a brick-and-stone stairway at the end of an entry road. The climb gradually draws visitors above the dust and noise, through a pomegranate orchard, to the top of the mound.

Standing on the rectangular, altarlike apex of the mound, we scanned the flat fields that stretched before us to the northern horizon. Only from here do you get a sense of the monument's awesome majesty and the immeasurable cost in human labor that had been marshaled to build it.

The great tumulus rises more than 140 feet from its base, which measures more than 1,100 feet on each side. It once crowned a lavish funerary park that in Qin times was named Mount Li Mausoleum in honor of the mist-shrouded mountain range that rises nearby. The bits and pieces of archaeological evidence so far collected suggest that an impressive complex of offices, walkways, and service buildings, together with a lavish temple, once graced the garden.

These structures were meant to ensure the perpetuation of ceremonies and sacrifices to King Zheng, the "Tiger of Qin," who before his death had assumed the grand title Shihuangdi, First Sovereign Emperor, and established a new dynasty. The tumulus was once surrounded by two walls — an inner wall with a perimeter of one and a half miles and an outer one with a perimeter of four miles. This configuration of enclosed space closely resembles that of Chinese imperial cities, with both a "forbidden" inner quarter and outer sectors on either side of the outer wall.

The First Emperor was a brilliant but tortured man who was obsessed with the fear of death. When he was not energetically avoiding assassination, he was searching for elixirs of immortality. How was it, then, that the emperor devoted so much energy to planning his tomb? Part of the answer lies in ancient Chinese perceptions of the soul and the afterlife. The *Li Ji*, or *Book of Rites*, compiled in the Han dynasty that succeeded the Qin, explains that each person has two souls: the *shen*, or spirit, and the *gui*, or ghost. The gui remains underground after death, while the shen flies upward to become a divine being. Different types of ceremonies were required to serve each spirit.

Tomb building was also a political statement. Even before Qin times, funerary design was a matter of great symbolic importance. The height of a tomb mound symbolized the rank of the deceased. Status had once been inherited, but increasingly it was the result of achievement. In accordance with the First Emperor's unique place in the history of his people, his tomb had to be the most extravagant ever seen — part of a massive building project that included expanding the capital at Xianyang, not far from present-day Xi'an, and constructing a new grand palace on the south bank of the Wei River.

Chinese court history tells us that the same laborers who excavated the earth covering the imperial tomb also raised the timbers of the emperor's E Pang Palace. More than 700,000 men, most of them convicts, apparently shifted back and forth from one project to the other. The emperor, according to one Chinese account, boasted: "This palace will have the capacity to entertain one hundred thousand men who will come by cart to drink wine and on horseback to warm their hands by the fire. One thousand men will sing and ten thousand will harmonize."

The great palace was not finished in the emperor's lifetime, but court histories record that he enjoys its replica in death. His earthly spirit was said to roam courtyards like those of the vast edifice — though on a smaller scale — that were reproduced inside his tomb.

The First Emperor, apparently determined to be First Ancestor as well, erected the Temple of the Absolute south of the Wei River. He dedicated it to the worship of himself and ordered it to be connected to his tomb and to the capital by arterial roads. Few indications of this construction survive.

Zhu Jian and I ambled back down the steps, past vendors hawking persimmons, warm buns, and Kodak film, and wondered what marvels might lie beneath our feet.

While there has been a considerable amount of probing of the grounds around the mound, the tomb itself has never been opened. Speculation as to its contents has been based on one source, the account of Han dynasty court historian Sima Qian, who wrote his monumental *Shi Ji,* or *Historical Records,* a century after the fall of the Qin dynasty.

The tomb may have been begun as early as 246 B.C., when King Zheng ascended the throne at the age of 13. Large-scale construction followed in 221 after the unification of China. Some records, along with the recent discovery of a stone-working site just to the northwest of the park, suggest that the tomb chamber is built of stone. Sima Qian's brief description of the tomb hints at dazzling contents. As the emperor had ruled the universe in life, so was he meant to enjoy it in death.

Within the tomb chamber, China's great rivers were recreated in mercury, which flowed by some mechanical means into a miniature ocean. Models of palaces and pavilions, constructed to scale, most likely duplicated those familiar to the emperor in life. Precious utensils and other valuables were placed in the tomb for his perpetual enjoyment. On the ceiling appeared all the constellations of the heavens, while the geography of the earth was represented below. Statues of officials paraded in imitation of courtiers in the imperial palace of the First Emperor's capital at Xianyang. The lamps that lighted this scene were fueled with whale oil to ensure that they would burn for the longest possible time.

The account continues by saying that the emperor, who died in 210 B.C., did not go to his tomb alone. Large numbers of childless concubines, along with laborers who knew the tomb's secrets, were compelled to join their ruler in death. To forestall looters, artisans were said to have prepared deadly traps that would fire crossbows at anyone so foolish as to enter the tomb chamber after it was sealed. As a final gesture, the mound was planted with trees and grass to give it the innocent appearance of a natural hill.

Later Han dynasty accounts, however, claim that few – or none – of the riches placed in the tomb survived the Qin dynasty. In 206 rebel general Xiang Yu reportedly ordered 300,000 soldiers to excavate the tomb and set fire to the surrounding buildings. His soldiers labored for 30 days to carry away the treasures of Mount Li. Whether that account is true or not, people apparently believed it. History records little more about Mount Li after that time. The Chinese people seemed to want no more to do with the place or with the regime that had created it.

The Tiger of Qin is as much a mystery as the tomb itself. In 238 B.C., having been king since boyhood, he came of age and strapped on his sword in an official ceremony. By then the kingdom of Qin, in an attempt to unify China, had been intensifying its campaigns against its neighbors for at least a century. The approach of ferocious and disciplined Qin warriors inspired terror. One history records that they received their pay only upon delivery of severed enemy heads. Other stories tell of warriors throwing conquered enemies into boiling caldrons and then drinking this ghastly human soup. These tales may be exaggerated, but the Chinese people knew that war no longer confined itself to a show of force by generals in chariots as it had in days of chivalry. Fighting now involved the entire population. When a town was put to siege and overthrown, no life would be spared.

The legendary ferocity of the Qin soldiers was overshadowed only by the reputation of their leader, King Zheng, who, after achieving military victory in 221, united warring Chinese kingdoms for the first time and announced the beginning of a dynasty destined to last forever. According to an inscription on a monument erected by imperial decree, "His influence knows no end, his will is obeyed and his orders will remain through eternity."

Qin Shihuang (as the emperor's title is often abbreviated) was one of the most innovative rulers of China and one of its most hated. Stories of his excesses and cruelties were embellished through the years. One of his ministers described him as "a man with a prominent nose, large eyes, the chest of a bird of prey, the voice of a jackal, and the heart of a tiger or wolf." This tiger, the Tiger of Qin, was ruthless and cruel, even by the standards of his own time. He trusted few people and was preoccupied with his fear of death. Nevertheless, his vision and his accomplishments changed China forever.

The First Emperor wanted to turn away from the past and make a world that was truly new. He unified and he codified. With the help of able advisers he extended Qin-style administration throughout the Chinese world. Feudalism was replaced by strong, centralized government. Some 120,000 powerful families, including former royalty, were forced to move to the imperial capital at Xianyang. To prevent armed insurrection in any of the defeated states, Qin Shihuang ordered all their weapons to be collected and then had the metal melted down and cast into bells and huge guardian statues for his palace.

The newly established empire was divided into 36 administrative units called commanderies. Each had a civil governor, a military commander, and an imperial inspector who was directly responsible to the emperor. Farmers were given rights over their land, but they also were subject to taxation. Currency was standardized to facilitate commerce throughout the Qin realm. Standardization extended to weights and measures, the writing of Chinese script, and even the gauge of cart and chariot wheels. Laws and legal procedures promised rewards for the loyal and grisly punishments for offenders.

The Qin system of mutual responsibility—which divided the population into groups of five or ten households and made each member responsible for the actions of all the others—has influenced Chinese bureaucratic style to the present day. The imprint of Qin administration marked Chinese civilization long after the dynasty was overthrown. But it was the excesses of Qin Shihuang that left scarring memories on the public mind.

The emperor and his prime minister, Li Si, considered China's ancient works of literature and philosophy—with their histories of previous kingdoms and moral strictures limiting the ruler's authority—troublesome and outmoded. The study of past methods of government might foster criticism of the present regime and so was, in fact, subversive to state security. Accordingly, in 213 B.C., Qin Shihuang and his minister began a literary inquisition that came to be called the Burning of the Books. Ancient texts are reputed to have been proscribed to the public, with the exception of those related to medicine, agriculture, forestry, divination, and the history of the Qin kingdom. Uncooperative scholars were punished by conscription or death. Popular myth insists that hundreds of them were buried alive.

All the public works commanded by the new emperor were built with conscript labor, but it was usually drawn from the peasantry. Besides the imperial capital, the E Pang Palace, and the monumental tomb at Mount Li, these projects included a radiating system of great new highways and the seemingly endless construction of frontier fortifications that probably linked existing walls built by the warring Chinese kingdoms. The unimaginable hardships these projects imposed earned their author the enduring hatred of the Chinese people.

Although Qin Shihuang founded an empire meant to endure for 10,000 generations, it outlasted him by only a few years. The Qin dynasty was violently overthrown less than four years after the emperor's death in 210 B.C. Members of the defeated nobility longed for the dynasty's downfall, and the common people despised the regime that had ruled them with such severity. A series of rebellions followed a soldiers' revolt in 209. Soon the once invincible empire collapsed.

"I don't like that place," one of my Chinese students told me after a visit to Lintong County. "It's too full of ghosts, haunted by the pain of the past." He echoed feelings long whispered by local people. Farmers who lived in Lintong told of monsters in human form that were occasionally unearthed by local grave diggers.

Suddenly in the 1970s, the ghosts of Lintong became the property of a much wider world. Given the nature of Qin rule, it seems appropriate that attention should come to the dynasty and to the emperor's tomb through the discovery of an underground army.

According to a sequence pieced together in 1984 by the *Baltimore Sun*, a group of peasants from a local commune were digging a well in March 1974 when their shovels struck what seemed to be an oddly shaped rock. By the end of the day they had unearthed a life-size clay model of a man's head with his hair pulled up into a topknot. Other pottery finds followed — more heads, together with arms and shattered torsos. At first, local people were unaware of the importance of what the well diggers had found. During the succeeding months, stories circulated about children carrying artifacts home to play with and peasants trying to sell clay figures by the side of the road.

At first, news of the discovery was kept to the residents of Lintong County. A local cultural center official visited the site and directed the digging. Farmers turned into instant archaeologists, and digging went on for at least a month without the presence of a trained archaeologist.

In June 1974 a Beijing wire service reporter, Lin Anweng, visited Lintong County. When he saw some of the figures, he was impressed by their beauty and convinced of their importance. Lin went back to the capital and wrote a special report about them. It came to the attention of top government officials in Beijing, and three days later the Cultural Relics Bureau was ordered to look into the matter. The Beijing officials instructed the startled provincial authorities to find out what was happening in their own backyard.

The timing was right. China was in the midst of a reexamination of Qin history and the role of the First Emperor. Mao Zedong, who, like Qin Shihuangdi, wanted to cast off the past, had no objection to being compared to the innovative First Emperor. By September, six months after the first pottery head was dug up, professional archaeologists had confirmed the nature and value of the find. The peasant well diggers had stumbled upon a life-size military formation — 6,000 armed warriors and their horses buried several yards underground. Their like had never been seen.

I first saw those figures in 1980, with friends from the University of Maryland. It was late in the day, and warm light spread across the reconstructed parade of clay troops and horses, battle ready again after more than 2,000 years. These soldiers suggest much more than military might. There is an elegance, even a serenity, about their faces that draws the observer to them. As we walked around the perimeter of the pit where the figures were discovered, restored, and set back in place, each of us instinctively located a favorite, one that compelled us to return to it.

Much has been said about the individuality of the faces. They may not be portraits, as some sources have insisted. It has been suggested instead that they were made from a number of different molds that produced partially finished heads. These were then hand-finished with special features such as hairstyles, beards, mustaches, lips, ears, and other details that give each face an individual look. Traces of pigment indicate that the pottery figures were originally painted in brilliant colors.

These terra-cotta warriors have prompted many questions. Why were the figures buried in this place? Especially, why were they located nearly a mile from the tomb? There is no mention of them in the historical record left by Sima Qian.

A number of theories have surfaced since the army was discovered. Chinese historian Lin Jianming argues that the array of clay soldiers and horses may not be associated with the tomb at all. Lin suggests that they were a kind of war memorial erected after unification. Such a memorial would have been an appropriate way to celebrate the emperor's victory over his enemies during his lifetime. Other people believe the warriors are standing guard over the First Emperor's tomb. But most specialists think that the clay soldiers were meant to protect the capital from attacks launched by armies from the six conquered states in the east.

Teams of Chinese archaeologists worked doggedly at the great pit to reveal and preserve its treasures. In 1976 discoveries were made in two additional pits nearby. They contained armed cavalrymen and kneeling archers, commanding officers and foot soldiers. At one time these troops had been roofed over and protected by timber frames like the one that had covered the first pit. But the wood had long since collapsed, causing massive but not irreparable damage to the figures. Not only soldiers were found in the three pits but also a wealth of military hardware. The bronze weapons unearthed in all three locations were real.

After three years of digging, the archaeologists paused in their work to analyze the riches they had found. They estimated that they would need 20 years just to excavate the first pit thoroughly. To protect the dig and to make it accessible to visitors, the area was roofed over and a museum created in 1979. By the early 1980s the pit received thousands of visitors a day.

Important Chinese ceremonial building was never a random affair. Structures on earth inevitably related to those thought to be in heaven, and symmetry was crucial. Discovery of the pottery warriors and horses to the east of the Qin tomb suggested that there might be other burials to the west. Several years of exploration have revealed this to be true. Further digging has slowly uncovered an expanding city of the dead outside the confines of the Mount Li funeral park.

In 1978 and 1979, excavations to the west of Mount Li exposed an entirely different kind of burial. Tradition maintained that 700,000 conscript laborers built the emperor's tomb. Now two burial sites revealed the fate of some of them. Near two villages, archaeologists located cemeteries for convicts who had worked on the tomb. In one cemetery, the bones of about a hundred people were uncovered, almost all of them young men. Buried with 18 of them were obituaries incised on tile, the earliest of their kind found in China. The tiles identified each person by his name and native place.

In 1980 came the discovery of two half-scale bronze chariots with horses, exquisite in detail. A parade of other finds included underground royal stables with lamps, shovels, and mangers. The stables held the remains of real horses, some of which had been buried alive.

East of the outer wall surrounding the tumulus, 17 royal graves yielded evidence of deliberate human interment. Examination revealed that men and women of noble families were buried there and had come to their end in violent ways. Some had been drawn and quartered and others beheaded or cut in half at the waist. These burials seem to confirm Sima Qian's account that Qin Shihuang's successor, his favorite son, disposed of all sibling rivals to the throne. Further discoveries include the remains of rare animals interred in clay pots, and of a kiln used in firing bricks for the tomb.

One particularly intriguing find is the location of an underground tunnel that archaeologists consider to be the main entrance into the tumulus itself. A smaller passage uncovered nearby appears to be an unsuccessful exploration by looters.

In 1985 Chinese scientists subjected the tumulus to electronic probes, accoustical soundings, and geophysical prospecting. They discovered an unusually high level of mercury in the soil—280 times that found in the surrounding earth. Do those rivers of mercury still run? This investigation leads archaeologists to wonder if the early accounts of looting could be wrong. Trenches dug in the immediate vicinity of the tomb show that its walls are intact and the earth covering them has not been moved. But the Chinese are approaching their exploration of the tumulus with great caution. There are no plans to excavate soon.

Meanwhile, the secrets of Mount Li are safe inside the tomb, and the Tiger of Qin walks the corridors of his palace undisturbed.

Armored and coiffed, ready for action, a terra-cotta archer kneels under the weight of his bow, long since decayed. Fragments of wood and metal remaining in the excavations show that all the soldiers' weapons were real. To create the army, Qin sculptors fashioned a wide range of armor and clothing. Bright colors once identified the men by units.

A reconstructed bronze chariot, fit for a ride through eternity, awaits the emperor's pleasure. Discovered in 1980 in a pit (left) near those holding the clay warriors, the half-size driver, carriage, and horses caparisoned in silver and gold testify to a high level of metalworking craftsmanship.

PRECEDING PAGES: Hoping to end the Qin march of conquest, an envoy from the state of Yan gained an audience with King Zheng by proffering a map of Yan and the severed head of a rebellious Qin general. A dagger flashed, and the ruler fell backward under the startled gaze of his unarmed courtiers. The attacker was killed, but repeated assassination attempts drove the king, when he became emperor, to a perpetual search for immortality.

*S*carcely distinguishable from gentle mountains to the south, the cultivated slopes of the Qin tomb rise above the lush fields of Lintong County. Han dynasty historical records claim that hordes of rioting rebel soldiers destroyed the tomb and

looted its treasures shortly after the First Emperor's death, but recent evidence questions the ancient record. Teams of Chinese archaeologists have been studying the tomb area since the discovery of the terra-cotta army in 1974. Probing continues (opposite), to determine whether more artifacts lie near the excavations. A variety of test results suggest that, contrary to traditional history, the tomb may not have been violated, and the fabled treasure of China's First Emperor may still lie undisturbed.

PAUL SLAUGHTER / THE IMAGE BANK (BELOW); CARL PURCELL (OPPOSITE); LEE FOSTER / FPG INT'L (FOLLOWING PAGES)

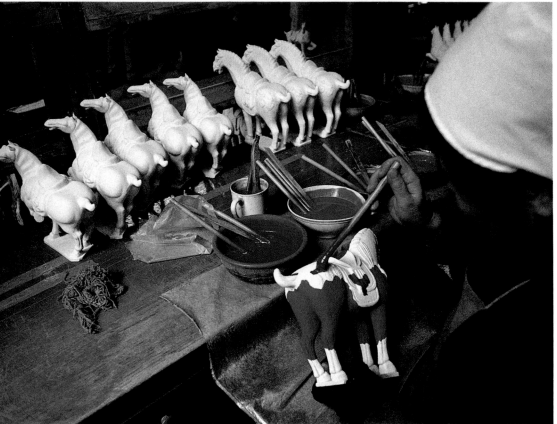

*T*okens of imperial splendor long gone, proud legions of spirited horses file in endless procession from kilns near the ancient capital city of Xi'an. The application of glazes replicates a style popular in the Tang dynasty.

FOLLOWING PAGES: Qin troops, as though on dress parade, march in the eternal service of their emperor. Painstakingly restored, these ranks of lifelike warriors hint at the wonders that may lie within the tomb itself.

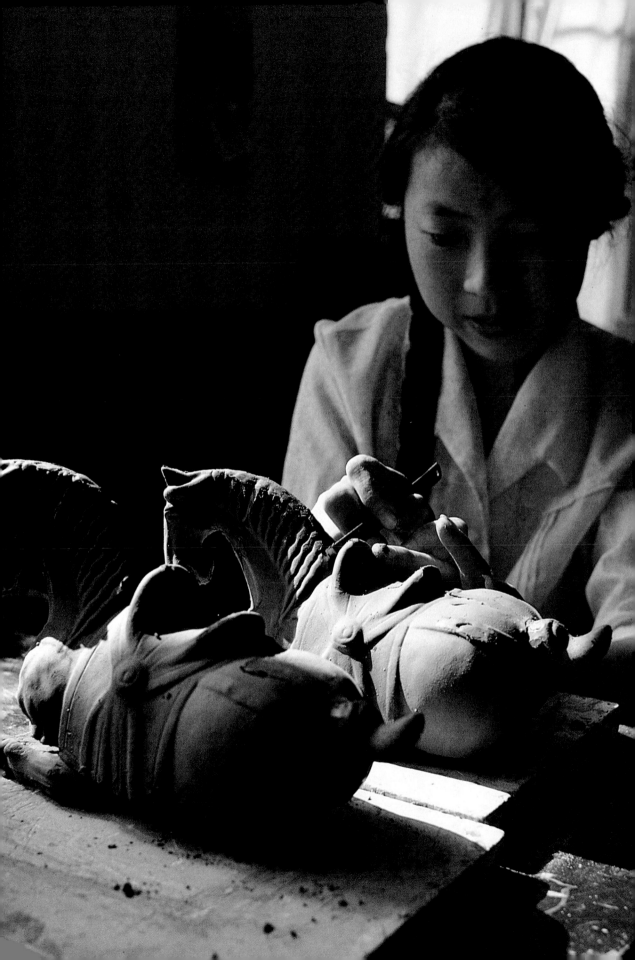

Easter Island

STONE SENTINELS

by Jo Anne Van Tilburg

I'm not a sailor. In spite of spending my childhood in Minnesota, "land of 10,000 lakes," I don't like the water much. All of my adult life I have lived on the California coast, safely planted on chaparral-covered hills, but well within sight and smell of the Pacific. It seemed to me like heaven, the perfect place, on the cusp of sea and slope. This changed in 1981. Suddenly islands — specifically Polynesian ones — became an important part of my life.

That year my work brought me to Easter Island, or Rapa Nui, the easternmost of the Polynesian islands. It formed when lava flows from three erupting volcanoes came together to create new land. Triangular in shape and only 62 square miles in area, the island lies some 1,130 miles from Pitcairn Island, its nearest inhabited neighbor to the west; South America is 2,300 miles to the east.

Since its discovery by Europeans in 1722, and despite a century of archaeological investigation, some writers have speculated that Easter Island is part of the mythical sunken continent of Mu. One popular author accounted for the large sculptures by imagining them popping, fully formed, from the mouths of fiery volcanoes, flying through the air, and landing upon conveniently placed ceremonial stone platforms.

I first traveled to Easter Island as an archaeologist with a University of California team to record prehistoric petroglyphs. Within days, my interest in the rock art was diverted by the carved monoliths scattered over the landscape. These sculptures, called *moai* by the inhabitants, were everywhere one looked, everywhere one walked. While I had expected to be astonished by the remnants of this island civilization, I hadn't expected to fall in love.

Facial markings prepare Carlos Pakomio for Semana de Rapa Nui. This festival honors traditions held before Europeans landed on Easter Island — Rapa Nui — in 1722.

PRECEDING PAGES: Star trails streak behind mystical statues erected on Easter Island. Ancient worshipers raised these moai *to link symbolically the natural and cosmic worlds.*

And that, I think, is exactly what I did. I fell in love with the boldness of the scientific challenge these statues offer — with their audacity in being so accessible, so numerous, and yet so puzzling. Most have fallen from rectangular stone platforms called *ahu,* upon which ancient rituals were performed by powerful priests and chiefs. Some statues lie on slopes, in ravines, or along ancient roads. Some are hidden, requiring long hikes and occasional descents into seaside caves to locate, but most are right in front of your eyes.

Over the past decade I have worked on an archaeological survey project sponsored by the University of Chile. My colleagues and I have measured, drawn, mapped, and photographed hundreds of these perplexing stone images. We can now address important questions about the statues and suggest answers. The questions people most often ask me are: Where did the people who live on the island come from? Who carved the statues? How many are there and how were they moved? What in the world did they mean?

The vast Pacific Ocean stretches over some 70 million square miles. So isolated and inconspicuous are most of its islands that from late 1520 to early 1521 Ferdinand Magellan traversed some 9,000 miles from South America through the heart of Polynesia and saw only two islands — and they were uninhabited. For about 14 weeks his fleet of three ships sailed before the warm southeast trade winds, and the mighty ocean he called Mar Pacífico was tranquil.

Such an easy passage, however, was dangerously deceptive. The trade winds swept Magellan's ships past and out of sight of the Juan Fernández Islands, Sala-y-Gómez, Easter Island, and Pitcairn, Ducie, and Henderson Islands. As weeks passed, the ships' limited stores of food and water became depleted and spoiled. Under the tropical sun, the demoralized crew began to hallucinate and then to die. Finally, the survivors landed, exhausted and in death's shadow, on an island historians think was Guam.

Magellan and other European navigators were relative latecomers. Centuries before, every habitable Pacific island and atoll had been discovered, settled, and in some cases even abandoned, as people we now call Polynesians spread eastward across the ocean.

Who were these great adventurers? For centuries the origins of the Polynesians were shrouded in mystery. Over the past 30 years, however, scholarship has revealed that a culture known as Lapita arose more than 3,000 years ago in Southeast Asia and is ancestral to Polynesian culture. From their ancient homeland, Lapita settlers and traders traveled to Fiji, Tonga, and Samoa. Many generations later, by the time great voyaging canoes left these islands to sail farther eastward into the Pacific, the people had become culturally Polynesian.

In the mid-1930s Rapa Nui people related their legends and genealogies to anthropologist Alfred Métraux. A modern version of their migration myth recounts how they came to Easter Island: "Our homeland Marae renga lay a distant journey to the west. There Hotu matua our king was one of the chiefs: Oroi was his rival. There was war between their tribes." Then Hotu Matua's tattooer, Haumaka, had a prophetic dream about a volcanic island with fine beaches, and "Hotu matua thought, 'There is a promise in this dream of Haumaka's.' He therefore sent away six men to find that land."

The journey to Rapa Nui was long. According to linguists, the distinctive tongue of Easter Island may have existed by A.D. 300 or 400, pinpointing a possible settlement date. Research by John Flenley, of New Zealand's Massey University, confirms that the island the Polynesian voyagers found was fully if not lushly tree covered. Legends say that the voyagers brought "the fowl, the turtle, the banana plant; the [paper mulberry] whose bark gives tapa cloth; the crayfish, the gourd, the kumara [sweet potato] and the yam." Prehistoric Polynesians were adept farmers, fishermen, and builders.

Given its small size, Rapa Nui has some startling geographic features. Rano Raraku, a volcanic cone in the southeastern sector, rises 490 feet above a nearly flat plain. The crater, holding a freshwater lake, is formed of consolidated lapilli tuff, a material suitable for sculpture. Another cone, 1,063-foot Rano Kau, lies at the extreme southwest point of the island. The freshwater lake within its caldera is nearly a mile in diameter. Here, high above the sea on the rim of the crater, the Rapa Nui people located their sacred village of Orongo, building basalt slab houses and carving hundreds of petroglyphs. Puna Pau is a small cinder cone located east of the present village of Hanga Roa. Its brittle scoria was used by the Rapa Nui for figures and for the distinctive *pukao,* or topknots, worn on the heads of some statues. The stone's color, the dark red of dried blood, is held sacred throughout Polynesia.

Both folktales and scientific research confirm that the moai were carved by accomplished, respected craftsmen called *maori* on Easter Island. Polynesian stone carvers belonged to craft guilds, and their skills, tools, and rituals passed from father to son. Their services were sought by important chiefs who paid for their efforts in food, especially greatly valued lobsters, eels, and large fish such as tuna.

An expert in any Polynesian profession is known as a *tufunga.* Tufunga included artisans in crafts such as house building and canoe manufacturing. Extraordinarily skilled individuals were believed to possess mana, or supernatural power. The East Polynesian god Tane was frequently associated with these crafts, and priests who belonged to appropriate guilds officiated at ceremonies and rituals in his honor.

Hundreds of heavy basalt carving tools have been recovered from nearly every part of the Easter Island quarries at Rano Raraku. Each time I visit the inner quarry, I am struck by its silence. Usually the only sounds one hears are the wind, the birds, and the distant waves. To conjure the quarry as it must have been, I imagine the resonant ring of stone tools against volcanic tuff. This underlying, rhythmic din would have been accompanied by the shouting and chanting of dusty men at work.

Quarrying methods used in Rano Raraku were similar to those used to cut coral or stone slabs elsewhere in the Pacific. Most often, a rectangular form was first roughed out and then undercut by work parties who stood in trenches around the form. Facial features may have been carved before other details, such as hands, were added. This would make sense; the heads were usually the most important attributes of Polynesian images.

Rapa Nui ahu (platform) architecture varies, but the statues show a high degree of standardization. This suggests that ahu were probably built by local groups of related people who used a preset plan, but varied the material, size, and style. The statue carvers, in contrast, were well organized and successful in teaching and controlling the work. The degree of technical skill varies, which suggests that some statues may have been carved as part of the master-apprentice teaching process traditional in Polynesia. Although each work party was probably under the direction of a master carver, there does not appear to have been an overall authority.

Throughout Polynesia, when a powerful chief wanted an object of great social and spiritual significance such as a sacred canoe – or, on Rapa Nui, a statue – an expert was engaged to produce it. After a formal agreement between the two, the members of the chief's lineage and others under his authority made the required payments of food. In this way, the sacred object became the property of the chief who commissioned it and of the lineage that supported the carvers with food. Often the object was also regarded as the property of the island's paramount chief. He had the responsibility of using all of his mana for the benefit of the whole island.

I worked alone in my first field season, usually traveling on foot and concentrating on the most accessible sites. The work was never repetitive, and the glorious weather was a joy. Felipe Teao, a wise Rapa Nui man of advanced years, joined me the following season. He taught me the Rapa Nui names of the statues, poked gentle fun at my Spanish, and knew the best trails through the rock-strewn terrain. Since then, the size of my field crew has grown, and in one season it numbered eight people. Two Rapa Nui artists have made drawings of many of the statues. Their insights into island ways have proved invaluable.

We have ascended rickety ladders in gusty winds and descended into dank seaside caverns in search of the ubiquitous moai. We have learned to beware of black widow spiders nesting snugly in the statues' ears and eyes, and to cope with the recalcitrant horses that carry us where there are no roads. And always, by the end of every day, we have learned something new.

This collective energy has allowed my Chilean colleagues and me to locate and describe 838 statues in the island-wide archaeological survey, which is nearly 80 percent complete. Ultimately, as many as 1,000 statues may be recorded. Of the 838 known statues, 396 are in the Rano Raraku quarry sector. Among these, 247 are in various stages of completion and range from $3\frac{1}{2}$ feet to nearly 71 feet in height; 149 of them had been extracted from the rock and stand on the interior and exterior slopes of the volcano.

The Rano Raraku quarries were first mapped in 1914, when British anthropologist Katherine Routledge spent more than a year on the island. Routledge explored the crater many times, pinpointing the statues and describing aspects of quarrying technology. She discovered that confronting the statues in their own environment was a humbling experience: "not till after some six months' study could they even be seen with intelligent eyes." One day, a member of her expedition, standing on a small hill overlooking the south coastal plain, was astounded to see the clear track of a statue transport road winding across the landscape.

Outside the quarry area there are 442 statues; 269 of them once stood on various ahu sites in the interior and on the coast. These regions of generally fertile soil were home to large numbers of Rapa Nui people. The smallest statue recorded on an ahu site is about 3 feet tall; the two largest are about 32 feet tall. Only one of these huge statues was successfully erected on its ahu.

The earliest date we have for a statue is at the ceremonial center of Ta-hai on the west side of the island. There, the head of a statue carved from red scoria was found in the bay. The platform with which it was probably associated has a radiocarbon date of A.D. 713. The time span for the use of red scoria statues on the island is enormous. Another red scoria statue found at a different site was known to be in use as late as 1868.

We have recorded only 49 statues that were not carved in Rano Raraku, but instead were cut from quarries of basalt, trachyte, and red or reddish-gray scoria. All of these statues are smaller than average.

Once carving was completed and before the final polishing was done, the statues were transported from Rano Raraku to ahu over the roads that Katherine Routledge's expedition discovered and that can still be seen today. These roads, between 9 and 13 feet wide, are really tracks of compacted earth. Most of the 47 statues we have documented along the roads lie on their backs, but a few rest on their faces or sides.

These statues lying "in transport" are perhaps the biggest unsolved mystery on Easter Island. Their varying positions mean that not all of them were being transported in exactly the same way. Their locations in relation to one another suggest that some lay almost blocking the roads while others were being manipulated to move around them. Routledge was the first to notice that some of these statues were broken in a violent way. She thought they might have been standing upright at one time and the breakage was the result of their falling to the ground. She concluded that some statues might have been erected to form ceremonial entranceways to Rano Raraku. Were the road statues standing upright, and if so, was this why?

In 1987 we began some exciting work that we hope will solve the mystery of the in-transport statues. The first step in understanding how the Rapa Nui moved statues was to isolate the average — the one most widely produced and most frequently transported. After every season of fieldwork, I entered measurements into a computer data base.

We discovered that the typical statue is rectangular, measures 13.3 feet tall, and weighs about 13.8 tons. This type was successfully transported and erected all over the island. It was probably preferred because it was manageable in size and weight, and the group of people required to move it could be easily assembled and fed.

Our next step was to produce a three-dimensional image of the average statue by using photogrammetry and computer drafting programs. Computer imaging allowed us to move our statue over mapped terrain, choosing the best route. We could now test various ways in which the Rapa Nui might have moved all of their statues to the various ahu.

We imagined that the Rapa Nui probably utilized generations of Polynesian expertise in marine exploration and canoe construction to develop statue transport technology. Principles of the fulcrum and lever were easily adapted to statue transport. So, too, were lashing methods and the production of strong cordage, as well as techniques of raising masts.

The islanders probably adapted a basic repertoire of transport methods to each statue as the need arose. The average successfully transported statue was moved horizontally and usually on its back, securely lashed in a protective wooden framework. Rollers or skids might have been necessary on some uphill or downhill portions of the roads. We calculated that fewer than a hundred people could have moved the average statue in this way. It seems clear that individual work parties of closely related people who lived on shared land moved single statues. Ancient obligations of family required that they participate. People outside this circle might have helped if the high prestige of the chief who commissioned the statue guaranteed substantial amounts of food as a reward for labor. Craftspeople and priests of high status and proven expertise would have directed these efforts.

Our work shows that the Rapa Nui chiefs had only a 10 percent success rate when they tried to move statues that weighed more than the average. A single statue of approximately 89 tons was the heaviest to be successfully transported to an ahu. This means that very few social groups could command enough resources to make the most demanding statue-moving efforts. The underlying social system obviously had a breaking point.

It is that breaking point, so dramatically illustrated by the 47 statues in transport, that we are trying to comprehend. Was Routledge right — were the road statues standing erect as ceremonial sentinels guarding or marking the approach to Rano Raraku? Or were they being transported standing upright, as some people have suggested? Had unsuccessful attempts been made to erect some statues temporarily, thus accounting for the breakage? Had others been standing for a social or ritual reason we cannot read in the archaeological record? Or, more likely, were most of them abandoned simply because the chiefs who commissioned them didn't have the ability to marshal the resources to move them? Were they just too big to be moved with the existing technology? For now, these perplexing questions remain unanswered.

There is no recorded evidence to help us understand how the statues were used in ritual. When Capt. James Cook explored Tahiti and Hawaii, he observed and even participated in ceremonies that incorporated god images. These were a vital part of religious beliefs. On Easter Island, however, neither Cook in 1774 nor any other observers before or since have recorded seeing a priest conduct a ritual in front of an erect moai on an ahu. In fact, Cook thought the statues were "Monuments of Antiquity" and did not believe they were worshiped by the islanders.

Besides a lack of firsthand observation, we face an even more compelling loss of data on Easter Island. After discovery, the Rapa Nui suffered severely at the hands of American and European whalers, sealers, and others calling at their impoverished shores. In 1862–63 the island was the target of slave traders, and the culture was dealt a murderous blow. Virtually all of the rulers and learned men were kidnapped and carried off to Peru as slaves. After the intercession of religious and other world leaders, the few Rapa Nui who survived were returned to the island with diseases that infected other people and ultimately killed many. In the wake of this tragedy, Catholic missionaries arrived to convert the population, and the remnants of traditional knowledge underwent further transformation and loss.

The work of scholars such as Routledge and Métraux is vital in reconstructing Rapa Nui culture in the years after European contact. The shadowy and mysterious prehistoric period is another matter, but fortunately we have some good guidelines. Captain Cook and other early visitors to the Pacific recognized the interisland similarities of peoples, languages, and cultures. Cook understood this and took islanders with him as interpreters. Polynesian religious beliefs and social practices on one island can frequently tell us something about similar practices on another. For this reason, better documented East Polynesian islands, particularly Mangareva, Mangaia, the Marquesas, and the Tuamotus, can shed light on their sister island, Rapa Nui.

Genealogies say that the Rapa Nui knew the great Polynesian gods and heroes Tangaroa, Rongo, Tu, Tane, and Tiki as legendary figures or divine ancestors of kings. During historic times, the greatest god of Rapa Nui was Makemake, born from a skull at Ahu Tongariki and incarnate in a small, dusky seabird called *manu tara* — the sooty tern. Makemake was the creator of humankind, and Métraux suggests that he was the Rapa Nui equivalent of the East Polynesian god Tane.

Tane was First Man, widely associated with trees, forests, and birds that dwell in the treetops. He served as patron of woodcarvers and other artisans. Many Polynesians believed he lifted the male sky from the body of the female earth to allow life to develop. Tane held his two cosmic parents apart by erecting wooden posts, or sky proppers, between them.

Props to hold up the heavens are called *toko* in New Zealand. In Tahiti they are called *pou*. The Rapa Nui word for pole is *tokotoko*, and pou refers to a column, post, or pillar. Most intriguingly, Métraux tells us that Toko te rangi, or Sky Propper, is named in the Rapa Nui genealogies as the 13th king of Easter Island. Polynesian chiefs were often metaphorically referred to as the prop around which society was organized.

The Easter Island statues as sky proppers would have elevated the sky and held it separate from the earth, allowing light to enter and fertility of the land to be achieved. Increasing the height of the statues, as the Rapa Nui did over time, would symbolically increase the space between sky and earth and would therefore ensure the greater production of food.

Such concern for fertility was warranted. Easter Island was completely deforested, mostly to create agricultural land, at varying rates in different parts of the island. Both Rano Kau and Rano Raraku had been entirely stripped of trees by about 800 years ago, and there were signs of serious soil depletion, overpopulation, food shortages, and other causes of social stress a few hundred years later. By 1500 the Rapa Nui people were undergoing major shifts in social, economic, and political alignments, although they were still erecting statues in 1600.

Rapa Nui traditions tell us that the ancestral chief, Hotu Matua, had divided the island among his six sons, each of whom then founded his own line. These branches, even though all of the Rapa Nui were related through the founding ancestor, were frequently at serious odds with one another. In the later years of Rapa Nui prehistory, competition for food became more intense on an island growing dangerously overcrowded, and archaeology shows that these tensions exploded at times into open conflict. Religious practices gradually ceased to center on the moai and increasingly focused upon the pan-island religious center of Orongo at Rano Kau and, to a lesser extent, on the ancient quarries at Rano Raraku.

The Rapa Nui had entered a period of uncertainty and probable bewilderment at what was happening to their world. In the midst of these trying times, they began to explore their beliefs, expanding and adapting them to their reduced environmental circumstances. They developed new strategies to entice, beguile, and seduce the supernatural mana of their chiefs, gods, and ancestors. We begin to see at this time some experimentation with statue style and material. For instance, there is a new emphasis on incorporating female sexual symbolism into statue design.

Another concept probably being challenged was the East Polynesian version of the "perfect chief," the sacred and all-powerful provider through whose hands, loins, and spirit the people could transcend the limitations of their island world.

Red scoria sculpture, with its long history of use on Easter Island, might be related to the legends of the perfect chief, who was known as Tahaki. He was clever, powerful, and virile, admired for his beautiful red skin. He sailed a great canoe called Rainbow and had the power to control the elements, heal the sick, and resuscitate the dead in battle. His status allowed him to achieve great weight because he had generous access to food, and his long nails were the trademark of chiefly idleness. His sparkling eyes became stars in the sky.

Some island statues, many of which appear to be very late, have symbols carved on their backs that represent sacred, chiefly authority. Some resemble a rainbow, a bird — perhaps the sooty tern — or a sacred loincloth. The exaggerated proportions and emphasis on the hands and elongated nails, the spine, the head, and the eyes reveal these features as focal points of mana.

As elsewhere in Polynesia, the statue itself was probably believed to be an empty stone vessel, perhaps a form of the perfect chief. Into this universal male form various gods and deified spirits of chiefs might have been ritually induced to enter. These summoned gods probably varied in the powers they wielded, and both statue design and ahu variation suggest that the most powerful gods required the most elaborate ceremonial settings. Perhaps Tane and Tahaki, or the Rapa Nui equivalents, were among them.

There are no simple formulas, no easy theories, no shortcuts to understanding the moai. We will probably never know with absolute certainty what these statues meant in the lives of the people who created them.

We do know that the ahu sculptures are not portraits of specific chiefs. They are icons that exemplify the Polynesian concern with genealogy, generation, status, and respect. Not only do they stand erect, visually separating earth and sky; they also symbolically unite the natural and cosmic worlds and provide access to them for both gods and humans. The moai thus mediate between earth and sky, people and chiefs, chiefs and gods.

Finely sculptured moai guard Ahu Nau Nau, a ceremonial site. Their topknots, made of red scoria from the isle's Puna Pau volcano, may denote the ritual center's high status.

FOLLOWING PAGES: Birthplace of moai, Rano Raraku cradles a head bearded with lichens. In all, 396 statues remain there at various stages of completion.

Moai erect and supine command a grassy exterior slope of Rano Raraku. Still attached to the hillside's living rock, a huge reclining figure with elongated ears measures nearly 71 feet—the island's longest statue.

Sooty terns inspired the talents of Rapa Nui artists on the ceiling of Ana Kai Tangata, one of Easter Island's many seaside caves. The remains of lava tubes, the caves hark back to the island's volcanic origins.

JAMES L. AMOS (BOTH)

Symbols engraved on a rongo rongo tablet (below) mystify experts, who have labored for decades to decipher Easter Island script. It *contains more than 1,500 signs. They may stand for key ideas or for sounds that helped prompt oral histories. Amelia Tepano Ika, one of*

Easter Island's famed storytellers,
recounts the lore of her people,
passing on to a younger generation
the tales of their island heritage.

*F*ractured eye of a moai reflects an ancient sculptor's imaginative use of natural elements. Red scoria from a volcanic vent forms the pupil, which is encased in white coral from Easter Island's rocky coast. Still standing on Rano Raraku, a haughty-visaged statue (opposite) is blind. The ancient islanders fitted moai with eyes only after positioning the figures at ceremonial sites. The Rapa Nui believed that the eyes gave the stone statues mana — supernatural power.

FOLLOWING PAGES: Replaced where they stood more than three centuries ago, seven moai rise from Ahu Akivi, one of the few inland ceremonial platforms on Easter Island. Restored in 1960, these statues never wore topknots. The island, now grass-covered or barren in spots, once supported thick forests of palm. Deforestation, probably through slash-and-burn agriculture, altered the soil, and perhaps hastened the collapse of the moai culture.

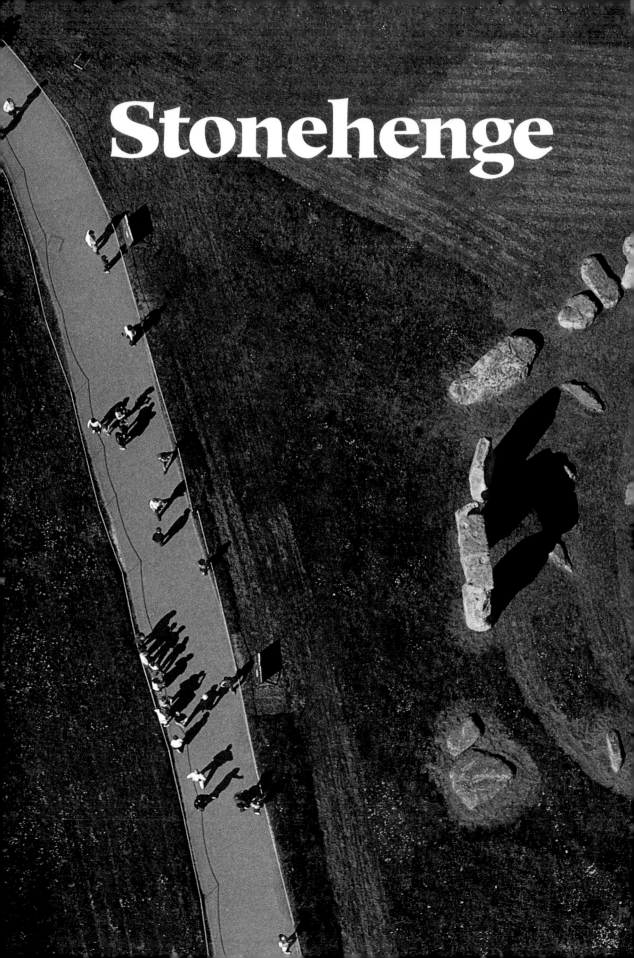

Stonehenge

SACRED CIRCLES

by Brian M. Fagan

S
tonehenge — its name is perhaps as famous as that of the pyramids at Giza or St. Peter's Basilica in Rome; but it is a simple, unadorned structure built of about 162 stones, and it stretches a mere 35 paces across. You feel less of the overwhelming sense of divine power and human insignificance that envelops you when you pause at the foot of the massive pyramids of Teotihuacan in Mexico, or under the soaring dome of St. Paul's Cathedral in London.

There is nothing very special about the location of Stonehenge. On my last visit to southern England, I stood on a ridge a mile away on a late summer's evening. The huddle of weathered stones sat dark against the stunted, dry grass of Salisbury Plain's rolling downlands, not in an amphitheater of spectacular hills, but near the top of a gentle slope. It was only when I approached and was a few hundred yards away that the stone circles stood out starkly against the setting sun. In the quiet of evening, the confusion of stones took on a deeper, more evocative meaning.

The name Stonehenge is of Saxon origin, a combination of the words "stone" and "henge" or "hang," a place of hanging stones, so called for the famous stone uprights with lintels that give the site its unique character. There are more than 600 prehistoric stone circles in the British Isles. None of them are as elaborate or were as carefully built as Stonehenge.

The exterior structure — the portion most familiar to us — is called the sarsen circle, so named because the uprights and their lintels are of sarsen, a durable sandstone. Within it is a circle of bluestones, named for their color. Inside this is a horseshoe of sarsens, and then a smaller horseshoe of bluestones. The so-called Altar Stone lies toward the rear of the inner horseshoe.

Self-styled "New Age gypsies" gather near Stonehenge's megaliths in the 1980s. Over the centuries the great mystical circle on Salisbury Plain has attracted all manner of devotees.

PRECEDING PAGES: Evening sun casts long shadows over Stonehenge. Scholars surmise that the monument took form in three distinct phases, over the course of 1,500 years.

This unique, primordial monument stands 330 feet above sea level in the heart of what archaeologists call prehistoric Wessex, a landscape of chalk grassland that was ideal for raising cattle and sheep and for growing cereal grains. It was here that powerful Bronze Age chieftains once reigned. The earthen burial mounds of these agricultural people stand out high on the windy ridges near Stonehenge.

Unlike Easter Island, Great Zimbabwe, and Palenque, which have been studied only since the 19th century, Stonehenge has been the subject of scholarly curiosity for more than 800 years. "Stanenges, where stones of wonderful size have been erected after the manner of doorways," Archdeacon Henry of Huntingdon wrote about 1130 in a history of England commissioned by his bishop. "No one can conceive how such great stones have been so raised aloft, or why they were built there."

Who built Stonehenge? asked the archdeacon and many after him. What was it used for, and what rites, if any, took place there? Had Danes, Romans, or Saxons erected the stones, or were they the work of mythical giants? No one believed that the "savage and barbarous" ancient Britons were responsible. Their priests, the Druids, according to descriptions in the Roman classics, worshiped in groves of trees, not among massive stones. Yet it was the Druids who would later become intimately associated with Stonehenge.

Two charming and slightly eccentric antiquaries first linked the Druids with Stonehenge. The first was the garrulous and energetic John Aubrey, who drew a hasty plan of the monument in 1666 and described it as a temple of "Priests of the most eminent Order, viz, Druids." Half a century later, Dr. William Stukeley spent the better part of four summers putting together "a most accurate description," with "nice plans and perspectives" of the site. He measured, sketched, and climbed a ladder onto one of the trilithon lintels, finding it large enough "for a steady head and nimble heels to dance a minuet on." He and his company even dined high atop the stones. Stukeley coined the word "trilithon" — from the Greek for "three stones" — that defines these freestanding structures of two uprights and a horizontal lintel.

The ever enthusiastic Stukeley was one of the first to realize that Stonehenge was part of a much larger prehistoric landscape of burial mounds, sacred avenues, and other features. He even excavated a double burial mound north of Stonehenge, where he found evidence of careful construction and a "rudely wrought" urn full of burned bones "crouded all together in a little heap, not so much as a hat crown would contain."

William Stukeley had been the first to point out that Stonehenge was oriented on the axis of the midsummer sun. "What can be more probable ... than that unlettered man in his first worship and reverence, would direct his attention to that glorious luminary the Sun?" he wrote. All the later astronomical theories that surround Stonehenge have been based on Stukeley's commonsense observation that the midsummer solstice was of cardinal importance to those who erected the great stone monument.

All would have been well if Stukeley had contented himself with publishing his sober observations. But he took holy orders in 1729, became obsessed with religious speculation, and transformed himself into an ancient Druid. He undertook to describe "the Religion of the Druids and all their Temples," tracing them back to Noah and the great Flood. The Druids of

Stonehenge, wrote Stukeley, were descendants of Abraham and had religious insights such "as should make our moderns asham'd." John Aubrey had been more severe on these ancient Britons. They were, he wrote, "2 or 3 degrees I suppose lesse salvage than the Americans [American Indians]."

"Stonehenge has never fully recovered from the Reverend Stukeley's vision," says archaeologist Christopher Chippindale, an expert on the history of the site. At summer solstice, modern-day Druids, acting out their exotic rituals in the heart of Stonehenge, were joined for a decade by an often riotous festival that featured sideshows and rock concerts. In recent years, British police have closed the site on midsummer's eve. In part because of Stukeley, Stonehenge is now under 24-hour guard, even in the depths of winter.

"How Grand, How Wonderful! How Incomprehensible!" 19th-century antiquary Richard Colt Hoare wrote of the standing stones in 1812. He sponsored digs supervised by another antiquary, William Cunnington, in the prehistoric burial mounds near Stonehenge; together they puzzled over the silent stones. These pioneers in the study of prehistoric Wessex excavated ancient barrows and passionately collected "the rude relicks of 2000 years"—some of them now on display at local museums. Prevailing scientific opinion still attributed Stonehenge to the Druids.

Until local landowner Cecil Chubb gave Stonehenge to the nation in 1918, the site was under siege daily from excursionists and casual visitors of every kind. We are lucky that its isolated location right into this century ensured its survival. "If Stonehenge had sat within a medieval village," says archaeologist Julian Richards, "then that village would now almost certainly possess some fine cobbled pavements and sturdy walls at the expense of the prehistoric stones."

Royalty inspected the standing stones; artists sketched and painted them; and British army regiments fought make-believe battles nearby. Some precariously balanced stones were propped up with stout timbers. In 1905 the Grand Lodge of the Ancient Order of Druids conducted a mass initiation of 258 novices in the heart of Stonehenge. The Most Noble Grand Arch Brother stood with his ceremonial battle-ax in front of an altar where a mysterious blue fire burned. Each blindfolded initiate swore an oath "as binding as sealing-wax, and twice as lasting."

Meanwhile, the megaliths went unprotected except for a flimsy boundary fence. Only once did an archaeologist excavate at Stonehenge. In 1901, William Gowland supervised the straightening of a leaning trilithon stone. Working with meticulous care, he uncovered broken flint axes and hammerstones that had once been used to trim the great stone. Gowland theorized that the sarsens had been moved on wooden sledges and rollers, then shaped with fire, water, and stone mauls at the site before being raised laboriously into position.

The first large-scale archaeological excavations began in November 1919. The British government commissioned the Society of Antiquaries of London to stabilize the monument. They put the work in the hands of Col. William Hawley, who stripped away valuable archaeological evidence from the entire southeastern quadrant of the site over the next seven years.

Although his excavations were generally a disaster, Hawley made a notable discovery: a circle of 56 round pits, which he promptly named after John Aubrey, the 17th-century antiquary who had been the first person to notice these depressions in the ground. The Aubrey Holes are straight-sided, flat-bottomed, and spaced at 16-foot intervals inside the bank and ditch that surround the sarsen circle. Some contain the cremations of humans.

In 1923 petrologist H. H. Thomas traced the source of bluestones at Stonehenge to the Preseli Mountains of southwestern Wales, across the Bristol Channel. The boulders, each weighing as much as four tons, had been transported some 200 miles to the site. The most probable route was over land and water, ending with the stones being rafted up the River Avon. It had now become clear that the builders had gone to extraordinary lengths to construct a unique shrine.

After World War II, archaeologists Stuart Piggott, Richard Atkinson, and John Stone went to Stonehenge in a serious attempt to dissect and date its long history. Collectively, they had vast experience in excavating prehistoric burial mounds and ceremonial sites elsewhere in Wessex. They also had a new archaeological technique at their disposal — radiocarbon dating.

Not that their experience made the task easier. They faced months of intricate detective work deciphering the notes of their less scientific predecessors. But, combining meticulous digging with careful application of the radiocarbon method, these archaeologists concluded that Stonehenge had first come into being about 2800 B.C., before the end of the Neolithic period. (Recent tests show this date to be about 3000 B.C.) The great monument changed and evolved over hundreds of years, just as medieval cathedrals have been altered and rebuilt again and again by generations of devout worshipers.

In recent years Julian Richards and other scholars have scoured the landscape around Stonehenge, trying to place the shrine in the time line of prehistoric Wessex. The story began about 4000 B.C., when farmers with herds of cattle and flocks of sheep first settled in the region. The rounded chalk hills and small river valleys of Wessex were once wooded, but the ancient farmers cleared them for pasture needed by their herds.

These early agricultural people had new and intimate ties to the land and to the seasons of planting and harvest. During the slack months they built elongated mounds flanked by shallow ditches that provided the soil for the tumuli. These mounds not only often contained burials, but, silhouetted against the sky, may also have served as territorial markers at the edge of cultivated land. Here, in this unremarkable environment, lies one of the densest concentrations of prehistoric sites in Europe. So diverse and unique are these settlements and ceremonial centers that we can be sure that Stonehenge lay in the midst of a landscape of great symbolic importance.

About 3000 B.C. farmers built a simple earthwork enclosure on a plot of cleared land at Stonehenge. This earliest Stonehenge was a cemetery, made up of a circle of small pits lying immediately inside the bank — the Aubrey Holes with their cremations. The first Stonehenge was used for several centuries, then abandoned before any of the bluestones or sarsens were erected in the center of the monument.

During this period of abandonment, while Stonehenge remained a relatively unimportant mortuary site, imposing ceremonial monuments were constructed nearby. These included long earthen avenues, stone and timber circles, huge earthen mounds such as Silbury Hill near Avebury, and a series of ceremonial enclosures known to archaeologists as "henge" monuments. The other henges differed sharply from Stonehenge. Invariably, a deep ditch lay inside an encircling bank, enclosing circular settings of stone or timber. At Stonehenge, the bank was on the inside, as if placed there to restrict access to the structures within and to protect them.

Many henges incorporated wood or stone uprights, but none except those at Stonehenge came from far away. No stones erected elsewhere displayed the quality of workmanship and such architectural refinements as shaped or jointed stones or horizontal lintels. And none of the other henges were used and remodeled over many hundreds of years.

By 2000 B.C. major social and political changes were afoot in Wessex. Before, local villages had been egalitarian communities whose residents were linked through strong kinship ties. Now individual power and wealth became all-important. Mighty chieftains gained sway in the rolling downlands. They were traders and warriors who, in death, were buried under round barrows in finery that included gold and bronze. Their ornaments came from far and wide—magical amber from the Baltic Sea and necklaces of faience beads from central Europe. Weathered carvings of bronze daggers fit for a chief can be seen on the uprights of Stonehenge itself. This was the period of Stonehenge's glory, of the constant remodeling and reconstruction of a monument set in an increasingly more imposing symbolic landscape.

About 2150 B.C. the axis of Stonehenge was shifted slightly toward the east to align the entrance with the rising sun at midsummer solstice. This orientation appears to have had a deliberate religious purpose. Around the same time, a ceremonial avenue facing the newly aligned entrance was begun. It consisted of a parallel pair of banks and ditches that ran cross-country for about 500 yards. Some archaeologists believe that inside the enclosure an incomplete double circle of bluestones faced northwest but was removed within a century. Opinion is divided on this. About 82 bluestones would have been needed to build these circles and to flank the entrance.

The greatest period of building activity at Stonehenge followed. Between 2100 and 2000 B.C. ten great sarsen stones, dragged from the Marlborough Downs about 18 miles to the northeast, were trimmed and set up in a horseshoe formation as uprights for five great trilithons with massive lintels. In addition, 30 smaller, but still huge, uprights delineated an outer circle. Their lintels formed a continuous, level circle 16 feet above the ground. Two uprights were erected at the entrance.

Standing in the heart of the sarsen circle, I have imagined the busy scene as local people raised one of the massive uprights. The great slabs lay on stout timbers after their long journey from the Marlborough Downs. For weeks a few skilled stoneworkers had tapered the 25-ton sarsens, using mauls the size of soccer balls. They had turned over the recumbent stones with large wooden levers. Then they used smaller, baseball-size pounders to smooth the tapered surfaces and to shape conical tenons for the lintels. Slowly, laboriously, they tapered the uprights and carefully shaped the gentle curves of the lintels that were to form an elegant circle atop the uprights. Stonehenge was to be special, the only stone circle where the builders erected a carefully fashioned architectural masterpiece that was designed to endure for many generations.

Meanwhile, other villagers were hard at work digging into the chalk subsoil with deer-antler picks, preparing a circle of deep, ramped holes for the uprights. Then, when the harvest was gathered and people had little to do in the fields, communities from miles around gathered to raise the stones.

A team of men rolled each stone for an upright to the edge of a pit, poising the base over the edge of the hole. They used massive timbers to lever the sarsen down the ramp and into the foundation. With much chanting and shouting, the team raised the great stone, inserting timber after stout timber under it until the upright was angled high above the ground. Next, they secured long vegetable-fiber or hide ropes to the top of the stone. While most of the team heaved and pulled, a few workers packed chalk, earth, and stones around the edges of the now upright sarsen.

Then it was a matter of fitting the curved lintels. Each village brought its share of long, thick timbers, while the elders supervised the construction of a wooden platform around two of the uprights. The villagers levered and raised the waiting lintel onto the platform. Day after day they added timbers to the rising platform, inserting them under the stone as they raised it ever closer to its final resting-place. Once it was on a level with the top of the uprights, the masons fine-shaped the mortise holes that would secure the lintel on the waiting tenons. Then they turned the stone over and levered it into place, adjusting the packing in the foundation around the uprights to ensure a secure fit.

The building of the sarsen circle took many years, for the people power available was never large and the task was enormous. We do not even know if the lintel ring was ever finished. One of the uprights, known to archaeologists as Stone 11, is thinner and narrower than the other sarsens. Perhaps this shows that the supply of massive stones was running out. Or could it be, as amateur astronomer Peter Newham has suggested, that the uprights of the outer circle represent the lunar month of $29\frac{1}{2}$ days, with Stone 11 being deliberately half-size? As with so much else at Stonehenge, we are left with impenetrable mysteries.

For the next 900 years or so, successive generations tinkered with Stonehenge, adding an oval structure of bluestones inside the sarsen horseshoe and later setting the stones in new configurations. Between 2000 and 1000 B.C., the avenue was extended in piecemeal fashion for another mile and a half, finally reaching the River Avon near the modern town of Amesbury.

The Stonehenge we see today is an amalgam of restless building that continued for some 60 to 70 generations. We do not know when this ancient shrine was finally abandoned. We do know that it was not a Druid temple. Contrary to popular belief, there is no evidence whatsoever that Druids worshiped at Stonehenge, for their rituals were more concerned with woods and water than with stone circles.

What, then, was Stonehenge? What prevailed upon Bronze Age farmers with only the most rudimentary of technologies to haul exotic boulders over long distances, to erect in stone a version of the elaborate circles their predecessors had built of wood? Was Stonehenge the center of some long forgotten religious cult? Or was it an astronomical observatory, its great stones aligned with the movements of the sun and other stars, as Astronomer-Royal Sir Norman Lockyer announced in 1906?

Most experts dismissed the observatory notion as ridiculous until the 1960s, when Peter Newham discovered new alignments for the equinoxes and for the moon at Stonehenge. Soon afterward Boston University astronomer Gerald Hawkins used a mainframe computer to plot the stone alignments. He found no fewer than 12 solar and lunar directions that, he calculated, would arise by chance with a probability of less than one in a million. Stonehenge was a "Neolithic computer," he declared.

Hawkins found alignments in the earliest, simple Stonehenge with its Aubrey Holes, which, he said, were used to predict eclipses of the moon. He also alleged there were less precise alignments in the later sarsen structures. Some controversy arose, since Hawkins, an astronomer, failed to use much of the archaeological evidence.

Newham and Hawkins had certainly shown the different ways in which Stonehenge could have been used to study movements of the sun and moon. But Hawkins assumed that any alignments he identified would be the same as those identified by the original builders. "This approach has pitfalls," says Christopher Chippindale. "You can, for example, use Stonehenge to calculate the dates of Passover and Easter."

Retired engineering professor Alexander Thom approached the astronomy of Stonehenge from a very different perspective. He set great store by accurate measurement and spent many years surveying stone circles throughout the British Isles. His figures convinced him that the circle builders had used a standardized unit of measurement, which he called "a megalithic yard" – approximately 2.72 feet. Not only that, but they also built circles in a series of standard shapes and often aligned them with stars or the directions of the lunar and solar cycles. Thom deliberately ignored the greatest stone circle of all, Stonehenge, until he had an unrivaled experience with alignments, circles, and other structures and their settings.

Thom came to Stonehenge in 1973. He began by surveying the entire monument from scratch with absolute precision. He and his team also studied the visible distant horizon, where the builders of Stonehenge might have located natural or artificial sighting points. Thom came up with two startling conclusions. First, when the main sarsen structures were built, Stonehenge was oriented on the half-risen solstice sun. Second, Stonehenge was an astronomical observatory. The stone circles were a central "backsight," used with no fewer than eight "foresights," mostly earthworks identified on the horizon around the monument.

If Alexander Thom was right, then Stonehenge surely was a highly sophisticated observatory, peopled by the "wise men, magicians, astronomers, priests, poets, jurists, and engineers with all their families" who, archaeologist Euan MacKie suggested, might have occupied such ceremonial centers. But, warns Richard Atkinson, it is folly to "abolish history, and to people the prehistoric past with ourselves in fancy dress."

Unfortunately, nearly all of Thom's "foresight earthworks" have since been shown to be of later date than the stone circle backsight. Despite his detailed measurements and lengthy calculations, Alexander Thom failed to reconcile archaeology and astronomy – to the point that few people now accept the idea that the Stonehenge people were expert astronomers.

Was Stonehenge an observatory? It is certainly a mistake to speak of Stonehenge astronomy in the same breath as that of the Babylonians or of the ancient Maya. No one doubts that Stonehenge was aligned on the axis of the midsummer sun. But the ancient stone circle was not a machine for measuring the sky. Nor were its builders in any way equivalent to professional astronomers. It was a temple that may have reflected the eternal, cyclical movements of the sun, moon, and stars across the heavens, but little else.

Why were such movements important? In many non-Western societies, the locations of the sun, moon, and stars still serve as vital indicators of the passing seasons. The Quechua Indians of highland Peru still observe the positions of the heavenly bodies by aligning them with jagged mountain ridges that stand out against the sky. Perhaps the priests of Stonehenge used their trilithons and simple stone alignments for the same purpose.

The people who lived in Wessex 4,000 years ago were in the process of coping with a demanding environment in which crops might wither on dry summer days, and animals could die by the dozen on cold winter nights. Theirs was an often difficult existence ruled by the passing seasons. Each spring the farmers planted the grain that was harvested after midsummer. Every year they witnessed the eternal cycles of fertility and harvest, of life and death, under the protection of their revered ancestors and in the midst of a deeply symbolic landscape. At Stonehenge their priests and shamans observed the passage of the seasons in the wide arc of the heavens and commemorated the cyclical reality of animals, plants, and humans with solstice rituals.

It may well be, suggests Julian Richards, that sunset on the shortest day of the year – the winter solstice around December 21 – was as important to these ancient farmers as the midsummer sunrise in June. Standing at the open side of the horseshoes on that evening, celebrants might have looked back into the monument and witnessed the midwinter sun sink between the uprights of the great central sarsen trilithon. As subsequent days began to lengthen, "the certainty would grow that the seasons were going to follow their natural order, spring would come after winter, crops would grow and life would go on as before."

One of the enduring fascinations of Stonehenge is that no one knows exactly why it was built. And therein lies one of the great unresolved mysteries of archaeology.

Rising out of the mist like a mirage, Stonehenge seems to float above Salisbury Plain. Some Elizabethans cited Merlin's "great skill in Magike" to explain the monument's creation.

FOLLOWING PAGES: Puddles of rainwater collect on a fallen sarsen. Huge lintel-capped sarsens frame the Heel Stone. Debate continues about how early Britons moved these stones.

*F*ollowing an afternoon storm, the
sky lightens beyond the craggy profile
of the Heel Stone. The stone acquired

its name from a 17th-century observer who noted "a cavity something resembling the print of a man's foot."

The rough, lichen-mottled boulder survives from Stonehenge's earliest phase, nearly 5,000 years ago.

Modern-day Druids celebrate the summer solstice at Stonehenge. Since the 18th century, Druid revivalists have sought spiritual inspiration in Britain's ancient circles. Official concern about damage to the stones has curtailed these gatherings in recent years. Once credited with

building the monument, Druids
actually flourished many centuries
later and preferred oak groves and
marshy places for their sacred rites.

*R*ays of the summer solstice sun crest the horizon, touching the Heel Stone and penetrating a lintel-capped sarsen portal. Some scholars have proposed Stonehenge as a kind of "Neolithic computer" for solar and lunar observations. Archaeological evidence discounts that theory.

*FOLLOWING PAGES: Snow encircles
Stonehenge, which still guards its
ancient secret: Why did Britons erect
this intriguing monument of stones?*

Medicine Wheels

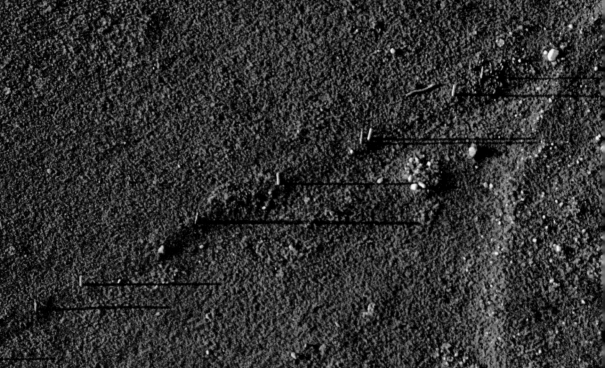

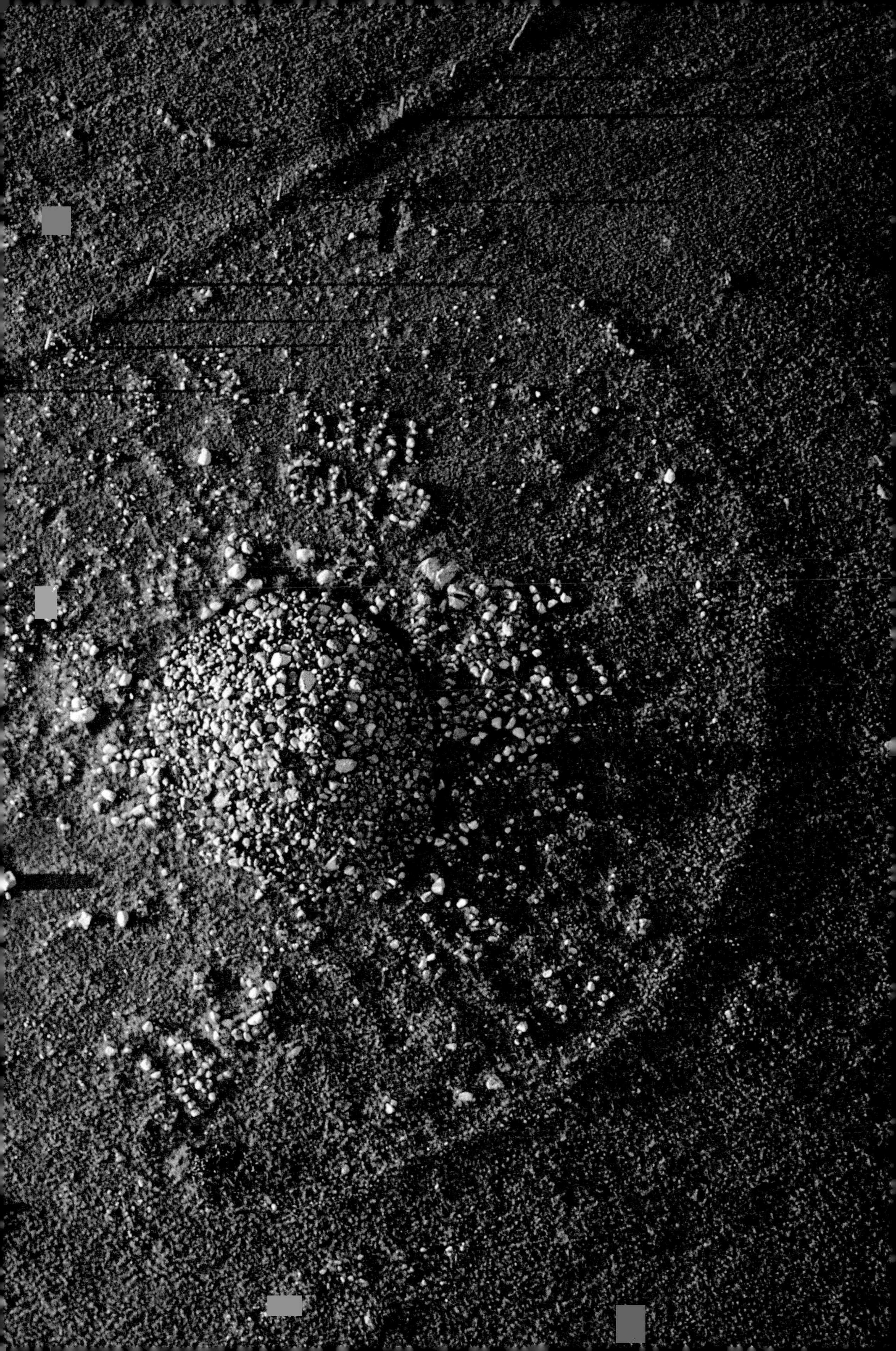

PUZZLES OF
THE PLAINS

by Tom Melham

The clouds parted just before sunrise. Lightning and thunder had ruled the night; now a slit of starry sky sparkled along the horizon, quickly fading with dawn's approach. Fog overflowed a distant ridge and tumbled downslope like spun sugar; a coyote yapped mournfully. Nonstop winds, chill even in summertime, clawed at me atop a narrow shoulder of Medicine Mountain, nearly 10,000 feet up in northern Wyoming's Bighorn Range.

Before me stretched a mystery: the Bighorn Medicine Wheel, a collection of stones arrayed in the shape of a wobbly wagon wheel. Twenty-eight spokes radiate unevenly from a hublike central cairn to a rim as wide as 90 feet across. Six more cairns sprout along or near the rim. The roughly piled stones create an impression that a couple of wiry fellows laid out the pattern on an afternoon off. White men first reported the wheel officially in the mid-19th century. Over the years it has mystified countless visitors.

Local Indians—Crow, Shoshone, Cheyenne, and others—responded to early questioners, "It was here before we came." Some tribes called it "the sun's tepee" and used it for ceremonies. Whites speculated: One suggested it was a Plains Indian model of the solar system; another, the ruins of a religious lodge. A rumor spread that 18th-century explorer Sieur de la Vérendrye had built the wheel as a memorial to Louis XIV, France's "Sun King." Phoenicians, Aztecs, even the residents of mythical Atlantis were implicated.

The term "medicine wheel" is, of course, a white man's metaphor. The phrase hints at some mystical use, for Plains Indians historically equated "medicine" with spiritual strength and even magical powers. But what, I wondered that dawn on Medicine Mountain, was the magic of this wheel?

Eagle talons, turkey feathers, and ermine pelts bedeck a Mandan boy at a celebration in Montana. Tribal elders teach that each item has a special "medicine"—spiritual power.

PRECEDING PAGES: Ancient, man-made bump on the sprawling Plains, the Majorville medicine wheel in southern Alberta predates an intruding fence by some 5,000 years.

Slowly, slowly, like lava oozing from a sleepy volcano, the sun's fiery head pushed above the horizon – and aligned perfectly with the wheel's hub and a second cairn, just outside the rim. I watched, spellbound. It was as though a great magician had conjured the sun to appear *there,* at a point of his choosing. And this was not *any* sunrise; today was June 21, the summer solstice, the longest day in the year. The spot of horizon now aglow before me was unique, touched by the sun only once a year. And, for reasons lost in the dim past, someone apparently had marked that spot with two rock piles, making Medicine Mountain a gunsight on the cosmos.

That evening I watched the sun set very near a point determined by the hub and a third cairn; this alignment, though not as convincing as the dawn's, was close. Thoughts turned to Stonehenge, England's megalithic circle that marks the solstice sun. Did the Bighorn Medicine Wheel serve its builders similarly, its cairns pointing out important celestial arrivals and its other features perhaps serving additional calendric functions?

I t's a tantalizing possibility, one that astronomer Jack Eddy first put to the test some 20 years ago. Years of research would convince him that the wheel's cairns marked not only solstice sunrise and sunset but also certain risings of some of the sky's brightest stars – Sirius, Rigel, and Aldebaran. He added that the number of spokes – 28 – approximated the number of days in a lunar month, and hypothesized how shamans might have used the wheel to predict stellar risings and measure summer's passing. To Eddy, the Bighorn wheel showed that Plains dwellers might have been far more aware of the universe's workings than anyone had dreamed. His argument grew more compelling when he surveyed another medicine wheel – some 425 miles away on Moose Mountain in Saskatchewan – and found that its cairn positions virtually mirrored those of the Wyoming wheel.

Archaeologists, however, did not embrace Dr. Eddy's theory. He was trained in the sciences of mathematics and planetary motion, not in Plains culture. And at both wheels a single cairn eluded explanation; no matter how Eddy paired it off, he found no alignment with any significant celestial target. Also, the cairns were crude markers, not pinpoint obelisks but sloppy doughnuts with central hollows and relatively large margins of error. Eddy suggested they might have supported slender poles that served as actual sights, but archaeological evidence for such poles was lacking.

The sophisticated astronomy that Eddy postulated for wheel builders had no archaeological support. Not one artifact of thousands found, not one interview of hundreds taken, indicated that Plains dwellers ever computed the sun's yearly travels. Yes, the Pawnee made detailed star charts; Cree "calendar men" counted off each month's days by transferring sticks from one bag to another; and many tribes had names for major constellations. But such things proved only that the Indians were keen observers, not that they predicted celestial movements. And why should Plains people *want* to track the sun or other stars? They were not farmers, like the corn-planting tribes of the Southwest, but nomads who followed the movements of their staple food – buffalo – and gathered wild plants. They had no need for a precise calendar.

Then there were all those other stone rings. The Bighorn and Moose Mountain sites Eddy focused on are but two of some 130 medicine wheels that dot the northern Plains from Wyoming well into Alberta and Saskatche-wan. They vary in shape and size — sometimes resembling stars, keyholes, or animals rather than wheels. In age they range from a few hundred to almost 5,000 years; many occupy overlooks commanding broad vistas. Some share astronomical orientations — usually to one or more of the cardinal directions — but that hardly makes them astronomical observatories.

Nor are these wheels the only enigmatic stone structures on the Plains. "Tepee rings" are by far the most numerous. These simple stone circles, usually no more than 20 feet across, once numbered in the hundreds of thousands — perhaps in the millions. Remains of hearths and other artifacts indicate that most were habitation sites, the stones of each ring apparently holding down the bottom edge of the tepee cover. But some rings occur near or on medicine wheel sites, suggesting that they and the wheels may have shared ceremonial roles separate from any utilitarian use.

Whoever made the earliest medicine wheels, it wasn't those supreme horsemen who dazzled Lewis, Clark, and other explorers. (The horse arrived with the Spanish in the early 16th century and took two more centuries to reach what is now Alberta.) Pre-horse Plains Indians traveled on foot, using dogs as beasts of burden. They were nomads who hunted bison in communal drives that relied on stealth and surprise. Over centuries, this area harbored different groups, some from the north, others from eastern woodlands. Tribal territories fluctuated amid constant competition and warfare. The arrival of Europeans on eastern shores sparked chain-reaction displacements as white settlers elbowed aside local tribes who in turn pushed neighboring groups farther and farther west. Despite ethnic differences, Plains newcomers assimilated resident traditions, sharing a fairly uniform Plains culture. Life-styles were molded by the natural harmony of the Plains — the awesome spaces, the ever dominant sun, the vast herds of game. The sun was the prime deity, symbolizing renewal and life's many cycles as it traced its daily and yearly circuits across the sky. Spirituality pervaded all; success in hunting, in battle, in life, relied not only on awareness of nature's ways but also on strong personal medicine superior to that of one's foes.

Like many Indian sites, most medicine wheels were looted by treasure hunters before archaeological work began. But even relatively undisturbed wheels have yielded little. Michael Wilson, an archaeologist at the University of Lethbridge in Alberta, visited the Bighorn wheel at the same time as Jack Eddy in the early 1970s and excavated part of it. He also has studied numerous other medicine wheels.

"There are a lot of loose ends," Mike says. "Every time you try to move ahead, you're stepping into another steaming pile of dragon manure and wondering what it means. Rather than solving problems, you're creating them. It's exasperating." Archaeologists, adds Mike, can't agree on what makes a collection of stones a medicine wheel. "This kind of wheel grades off into effigies; that kind grades into tepee rings; another grades into cairns. I'm bothered by the possibility that, to its builder, a big cairn without an outer circle might mean exactly the same thing as a medicine wheel. At what point does that outer line fade to insignificance? Where do we draw the boundary?"

Over several days, Mike, Neil Mirau, one of Mike's graduate students, and I visited six medicine wheels in Alberta. One was built especially low, its spokes and cairns barely visible until we were almost on top of it. "I'm not sure it was intended to be really evident to anybody," said Mike. "Maybe nobody on the ground needed to see it. Maybe its lines were meant only for the Creator and had no role, no value as messages to people."

He added that Indians extend symbolism to the most functional objects. The tepee ring is one example: "That's very utilitarian. But tepee rings are nice, careful circles. Somebody took care to make sure that when the stones were rolled back, they weren't just jumbled on the landscape. You have to ask, what other function could they have had?"

Were some wheels territorial markers? Or were they memorials that recalled a battle or other event, or perhaps an exceptional leader? More than a decade ago, Blackfoot Indians told archaeologist Thomas Kehoe that certain medicine wheels marked the death lodge sites of war chiefs; the spokes related to deeds of the departed. Of all nomadic Plains tribes, the Blackfoot held the same territory for the longest time; their death lodge explanation for the wheels may stem from earlier wheel builders.

Another theory ties medicine wheels to the all-important buffalo hunt. Keyhole-shaped wheels resemble drawings of historic buffalo pounds — corrals used to direct stampeding animals or hold captured ones. Might their design have engendered mystical power and thus ensured a successful hunt? Mike Wilson points out that even some round medicine wheels have a bison connection. For example, a 5,000-year-old one near Majorville, Alberta, yielded ceremonial pipes, beads, bits of pottery, and *iniskim* — tiny, buffalo-shaped stones that served as ceremonial charms to "call" buffalo within the hunter's reach. "Sites like this," Mike said, "have strong links with buffalo. You have iniskim, you're in prime buffalo territory, on heights of land with incredible views over broad areas where buffalo would congregate. Perhaps this wheel related directly to a hunt; perhaps it was used for a periodic ceremony of renewal that called the buffalo to maintain relationships."

Mike noted that rainfall determines the best buffalo country. Local weather records showed him that in the northern Plains, spring rains build gradually through June, then drop off. This finding evolved into a possible explanation of why some medicine wheels mark the solstice: because it means rain. For many Plains dwellers, the year's heaviest rainfall occurs around the solstice in late June. What if, Mike asked, wheel builders linked a ceremony to those rains — which were crucial because they meant new forage that would attract buffalo? Suppose they built a ritual structure oriented to sunrise on the day of the ceremony — a common Indian practice, even for tepees. To us, such an orientation would seem to align with the solstice — though the sun's position was of secondary importance. Mike had found a context to explain some of Eddy's solstice data.

George Bird Grinnell, one of the first anthropologists to examine the Bighorn wheel, noted that in the early part of this century Indians told him it was a stone version of the wooden Sun Dance lodge.

Sun Dances were midsummer Plains rituals that varied from tribe to tribe. They marked the new year and often involved self-mutilation and self-denial. Chief participants stared at the sun all day without shade or water or rest, in hope of appeasing the Creator and guaranteeing themselves strong medicine in the year ahead.

"A lot of the ceremony," says Mike Wilson, "was actually thanking the Creator. It looked backward and forward; it was a renewal." Does he consider the Bighorn wheel a good site for a Sun Dance?

"It's a powerful location—the way it's laid out, the fact that it has a designated center. It gets a lot of storms, and it's an eerie place. When you sit there for days—as we did when we excavated there—you soon learn that the wind shrieking through those dolomite clefts on the west cliff has *voices*. It sings to you. There are times when you'll almost swear you've heard a word. There's no doubt in my mind that spiritually it's a very powerful place."

Close by the wheel a series of natural caves and fractures adds to this location's mysterious aura. Exploring them, Mike noticed some "rock art" on the walls—that turned out to be natural shadow patterns that come and go as the sun passes over the rock entrances. He was fascinated.

"You see, there are traditions of 'Little People' who lived underground and came up to impart knowledge. The Crow talk about them, and I've often wondered whether ceremonies at this medicine wheel involved people coming out of an underground cave or retreating into it, perhaps to do some rite that shouldn't be seen by everyone. There's an analogy in the Sun Dance itself: At times, medicine men go behind a screen at the back of the lodge to perform certain activities; not all of them are public."

Mike says the Bighorn wheel "probably wasn't built all at once. Maybe as it grew, its function also evolved. Like the Sun Dance; it probably didn't spring fully formed from a conch shell, but grew from a simpler ceremony."

Bighorn's cairns—some ringlike, some even U-shaped—enclose cavities just big enough to hold a crouching human. Might they have served some use in a Sun Dance or other rite—perhaps even harboring 'Little People'? But Sun Dances were large, prolonged, communal events; Medicine Mountain impresses many archaeologists as too exposed and remote for such ceremonies. Some feel it served instead as a vision quest site.

Many Plains tribes practiced vision quests, in which individuals underwent fasting and other deprivations to attain mystical dreams or visions. Unlike gregarious Sun Dances, vision quests were private, pursued alone in a remote spot exposed to the elements and the universe. Many medicine wheel locations seem ideal for such a purpose. Medicine Mountain, for example, rises on the western edge of the Bighorns, which stand out as relatively titanic blips upon the Plains' flat table. They command spectacular views and experience rather wild weather. Local tribes have long considered them sacred. Perhaps Medicine Mountain's cairns once served vision questers as spartan shelters. But why seven cairns for a solitary experience? The vision quest theory doesn't explain other wheel features, either, nor does it illumine what its builders believed. Says Mike Wilson, "After a while, all medicine wheel hypotheses start to sound like a multiple-choice exam. You know, I'm beginning to believe the answer is 'all of the above.' "

Will science ever solve the riddle of the wheels? Neil Mirau doesn't think so. "The cultural gap is too great. Perhaps some day we'll understand superficially what medicine wheels were used for, but I don't think we'll grasp their entire meaning within the native universe. We live in our world; they lived in theirs. Our appreciation of them can never be complete." Mike agrees. "There's a wall," he said. "It's not just this word translating into that word, it's made up of different concepts, different thoughts. We talk of how 'seeing is believing.' But the existence of spirits is determined from within. You must believe in them to see them."

A historian can tell a Cheyenne that his ancestors couldn't possibly have built the Bighorn wheel because the Cheyenne were latecomers to Wyoming. But this simply doesn't translate. Indian time is not linear; despite historic "facts," a person can be almost anywhere at any time—in spirit.

Lately, the Bighorn site has gained yet another layer of spirituality: New Age prophets have adopted it as a "primary power center" of the universe. Boone Vuletich, an employee of the U.S. Forest Service, which oversees Medicine Mountain, told me: "We've had all kinds up there for summer solstice. I've talked to people that claimed to see little demons and gremlins and stuff; some believe it's a landing place for UFOs. Once I pulled a guy out of there wearing a steel-wool blanket and holding up a big piece of metal conduit, waiting for lightning to hit him so he could 'absorb the energy.' "

Then there was the nude woman he found inside the wheel, who informed him she was a 640-year-old witch. Recalled Boone with a wry grin, "We get a lot of people like that."

So it was that, on my recent solstice visit to the Bighorns, I anticipated a circus. The steel fence barricade was bedecked with modern talismans: a quartz crystal, bits of bandanna and yarn, feathers, a key on a string. Yet the solstice dawned with a mere handful of people—none of them New Agers—gathered quietly at the cairns. A couple of grandmothers from South Dakota had driven in the night before, because they "just always wanted to see it." Several youths had come seeking adventure and, perhaps, themselves. Three Crow Indians, from the nearby reservation in Montana, completed the group. They talked openly but anonymously, stressing that they represented not the tribe but merely themselves. Their purpose was simple: "We come to pray. Several times a year here, but always this time. It's a special place, a holy place. We just come to pray, to give thanks. Then we go home."

I left them in peace, standing directly in line with the cairns that pointed straight at the rising sun. Overhead, a lone crow hung nearly motionless in the sky, its wings outstretched in updrafts that continuously race over the mountain's western cliffs. It soared awhile, then edged forward, caught a new blast, and rose to its original position. Again and again it repeated the cycle. I thought of other wheels I'd seen, of the people I'd interviewed and the explanations proposed for these sites. I knew that I—like this bird—had come full circle; the mystery of the medicine wheels remained intact.

Two cairns of Wyoming's Bighorn Medicine Wheel seem to align with the rising sun on the summer solstice. Experts disagree over who built the structure—and why.

FOLLOWING PAGES: Craggy slopes guard the southwestern approach to the Bighorn wheel. The site offers spectacular views of the Bighorn Basin and the distant Rockies.

TOM MELHAM, NGS STAFF; DAVID MUENCH (FOLLOWING PAGES)

*H*emmed in by man and nature, Wyoming's Bighorn wheel (opposite) lies between a visitor parking area and crumbly, eroding cliffs. Scientists have put forth numerous theories — ranging from celestial alignments to Sun Dance ceremonies — to explain the wheel's odd collection of 7 cairns and 28 spokes, and they argue, too, over its original purpose. The wheel's ageless allure inspires imitators even today; a tiny satellite structure visible in the middle foreground bears witness to the actions of recent wheel builders. Other visitors hope to tap into the wheel's medicine by bestowing various talismans upon the site's protective fence (below).

JEFF HENRY; COMSTOCK / GEORG GERSTER (OPPOSITE)

*T*all on tradition, a Shoshone youth courses the Plains bareback, as did his ancestors. An unintentional gift to the New World from Spanish explorers, the horse transformed Plains Indians from footbound hunters and gatherers into highly mobile nomads. Tribal ranges waxed and waned dramatically long before white men reached the Plains. Crow, Northern Cheyenne, and Shoshone occupied Wyoming and southern Montana in historic times, and today all claim the Bighorn wheel as their own. But no Plains Indians could (or would) tell 19th-century interviewers who built it.

DAVID STOECKLEIN / THE STOCK MARKET

*P*asqueflowers brighten the northern Plains in spring, when seasonal rains encourage the new growth of grasses that nourish bison (opposite), once the staple of all Plains Indians.

FOLLOWING PAGES: Buffalo hide has given way to canvas, but tepees still dot the Montana landscape at an annual Crow gathering, recalling the enduring Plains Indian culture.

GEORGE WUERTHNER (ABOVE); LOWELL GEORGIA (OPPOSITE);
ROY MORSCH / THE STOCK MARKET (FOLLOWING PAGES)

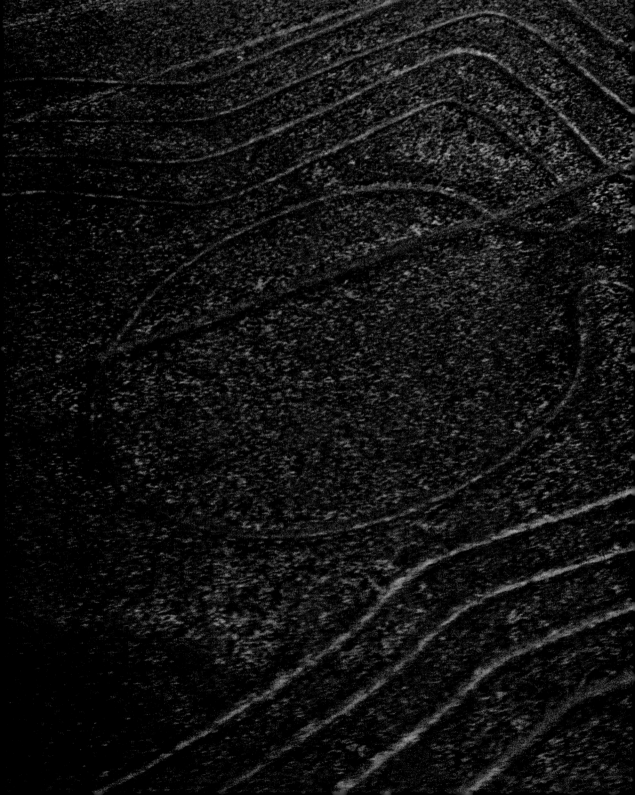

Nazca Lines

PATTERNS ON THE DESERT

by Anthony F. Aveni

Whoever built the Nazca lines in the Peruvian desert intentionally altered the earth's surface on a grand scale for no reason that makes immediate sense to us. At least we can comprehend the Egyptian pyramids as works of architecture. But the abstract look, the geometric proportions, the beauty combined with precision, and the gigantic scale of these mysterious lines leave us wondering: Who made them? When were they made, and why?

Like all famous mysteries about which we have few facts, there is no shortage of explanations for the markings on the southwestern coastal desert plain between the Nazca and Ingenio Rivers—the Nazca pampa. Answers come from everywhere and everyone. From artist to engineer, theologian to astronomer, anyone who has paid $100 to make the 40-minute tourist pilgrimage in a rickety Cessna ends up back at Nazca's dusty airport not only with nausea but also with a firm opinion.

For some people the lines are signals to ancient extraterrestrial astronauts, even runways for them to land on should they contemplate a return visit. For others the zigzag figures might be ancient Olympic running tracks. The pampa could be the world's largest map, a huge plan ten miles on a side indicating pan-Andean trade routes; or a tidal calculator; or perhaps the world's biggest astronomy book, plotting important constellations. Or is it a stellar template, an analog star map that locks each effigy on the pampa surface into real star patterns at certain times of the year? Could it have been an unwritten calendar that told when to plant, harvest, or irrigate? Could you judge these dates, for example, by standing on the proper line at the correct time of the season and looking along it to the horizon to see where the sun

Stone-lined spiral ojo — "eye," in Spanish — marks a reconstructed well near Nazca. Such shafts formed part of a system of aqueducts that tapped subsurface water for irrigation.

PRECEDING PAGES: Gigantic spider, 150 feet long, dwarfs researchers. Why the ancient Nazca etched such outsize figures and geometric designs on the pampa intrigues scholars.

would rise or set? That is apparently what American geographer Paul Kosok thought when he wrote: "With a great thrill we realized at once that perhaps we had found the key to the riddle." He and his wife, Rose, were on a picnic and had just witnessed the sun setting along one of Nazca's straight lines on the first day of winter 50 years ago.

To find an answer, scientists usually begin by classifying. Should we put the lines in the same compartment as effigy mounds — earthworks such as the Hopewell Serpent Mound in Ohio — or are they more like modern earth art? I think of Nancy Holt's plan for "Sky Mound," which will turn a landfill in New Jersey into an artwork of radiating paths, tunnels, posts, and mounds that align with the sun, moon, and two major stars on important astronomical dates. Such modern earth art has its ancient counterpart in England's Uffington White Horse, made by Iron Age people who scraped away the turf to expose chalk, thus etching the stark white outline of the revered animal.

I f you want to get a handle on the Nazca lines, you need to come down out of the clouds. The lines were made on the earth by people who lived on the earth. And anyone who wishes to become familiar with these ancient artifacts needs to get out on the hot, arid pampa and spend time carefully studying the remains piece by piece. You also need to understand the culture of Nazca and those of the Andes in general. This was the philosophy of our research group when we worked on the pampa between 1981 and 1984. The group included anthropologists Gary Urton of Colgate University and Tom Zuidema of the University of Illinois, archaeologists Helaine Silverman, also of Illinois, and Persis Clarkson of the University of Winnipeg in Canada, and me, an astronomer at Colgate. We were assisted on several occasions by the volunteer organization Earthwatch.

From above, the desert looks like a classroom blackboard at the end of a very busy day — a day when the janitor was out sick! But from the ground, the lines can be systematically untangled. You can walk, measure, and map them. Only then do patterns on the desert begin to emerge.

There is a total of about 800 miles of straight lines, and we have cataloged 762 of them, or about 90 percent. There are approximately 300 geometric figures, mostly trapezoids and triangles. Their dimensions are truly colossal: They average about 1,300 feet long and 130 feet wide at the base. Often they are clipped off at the apex, and long, thin triangles or lines, some running perfectly straight for miles, seem to be appended to them.

There are also zigzag scrawls, spirals, and some three dozen figures taken from nature: many birds, a few fish, a monkey, a spider, and a small number of weird plants. Though the animal figures are well-known, most are relatively small; one hummingbird is about 330 feet long, roughly the same as the wingspan of the condor and the length of the monkey, with its coiled, labyrinthine tail. The long-necked bird, probably a cormorant, is the longest of the creatures, measuring almost 2,000 feet from beak to tail feathers.

Nearly all of these animal and plant figures are confined to a 4-square-mile strip of the pampa near the Ingenio River. But geometric figures, totaling 4.3 million square yards in area, are etched across the entire 85-square-mile pampa. The pampa is otherwise unmarked except where river tributaries, usually dry, flow northeast to southwest and dry washes erode the surface.

I think of the lines as etchings because they were made by a process of subtracting material from an existing medium. The etching of a line involved the removal of the fist-size pieces of desert-varnished, or oxidated, rock that coat the pampa. Occasional flooding, often induced by heavy summer rains, had swept these chunks down from the Andes hundreds of thousands of years ago. The delicate ecology of this narrow strip of arable land lying between coastal and montane environments depends on seasonal events that occur a day's walk away. Thus, the water that runs on the pampa does not fall directly from the skies. Rather, it rolls down in torrents from the high mountains to the east. Looking from the pampa, one can see the welcome dark clouds that enshroud the Andes, portending the arrival of precious rain.

The exposure of the lighter, unoxidized undercoating of sand, along with a black edging of neatly piled detritus around the cleared area, renders each figure distinctly visible. Clues to the method of construction come from some lines that for unknown reasons were left unfinished more than a thousand years ago. Our survey disclosed numerous piles of stones in the middle of partially cleared figures and conveniently located about an arm's length from one another. I speculate that the fragments had been gathered into neat piles by teams of workers who squatted there; the piles were then likely removed to the borders where the edging process—the careful lining up of cleared stones to form the outlines—would proceed. Today, native farmers in the adjacent valley still clear their cotton fields by this orderly method of removing and piling stones.

The statistics may stagger the imagination, but the Nazca lines are not improbable feats of engineering such as, for example, the pyramids of Egypt. Nor would one have needed an advanced technology to construct them. On a remote area of another pampa in June 1984, 12 Earthwatch volunteers, with neither a printed plan nor measuring equipment, constructed a straight line 115 feet long and $2\frac{1}{2}$ feet wide that ended in a spiral. They used the hypothetical construction method supported by pampa remains. One crew sighted the edges of the line using a distant hill and laid out the borders with ropes and sticks. Then members of another group, spaced an arm's length apart, squatted in the interior collecting the stones into piles. A third group removed them to the edges and arranged them in neat hummocks. They followed the instructions of the "elite" group on the hill who, never needing to bend over, supervised the edging process to be sure things lined up correctly. The result was a line as accurate as any we measured with a surveyor's transit. Total work time: an astonishingly brief 90 minutes!

We concluded that our volunteers could have cleared an average-size trapezoid—an area of 19,000 square yards—in about a month, and that a combined labor force of 10,000 people working a 40-hour week could have executed every line and trapezoid on the entire pampa in a few decades. Later, we erased our "Earthwatch Spiral" so as not to confuse archaeologists of the future.

The Nazca lines required no astronauts. There were people right there to do the job; archaeologists know of more than 500 habitation sites dating from 500 B.C. to A.D. 1500 in the green valleys that straddle the pampa. Helaine Silverman has mapped and surveyed many of these sites, and has excavated at the monumental religious center of Cahuachi, where she cataloged more than 40 structures. Cahuachi sits on the south bank of the Nazca River, just opposite the heaviest concentration of lines, and this, in part, led Silverman to believe that it once was a pilgrimage center, where groups of farmers congregated to perform religious ceremonies.

Cahuachi today reveals eroding adobe walls scarcely discernible from desert hills. Dating from about 100 B.C. to A.D. 400, the site had a number of temples, enclosures and plazas, adobe pyramids, and hundreds of burials, now mostly looted. The tomb robbers left human skulls, teeth, hair, even skin-covered bones, scattered on the surface.

The ancient Nazca people were loosely organized, living in large groups of extended families in a culture that flourished between 100 B.C. and A.D. 600. They were expert artists, and their colorful pottery is the predominant archaeological item that defines the Nazca culture. On some pots, outlined in black, we find birds, plants, monkeys — the same creatures sketched on the gigantic drawing board of the pampa.

Silverman's data and pottery sherds collected by Persis Clarkson from the lines, along with radiocarbon dating of organic material sealed within or beneath desert varnish on the rocks along the edges, seem to confirm that the Nazca lines were indeed the work of the Nazca people.

So we think we know how the lines were built, who built them, and when, but, while we can offer statistics on their sheer number and gross dimensions, a persistent question still attracts us to them: *Why* were they built?

I t's a long way from Cuzco to Nazca — about 300 miles by rough road, in fact. In August 1977 — winter in South America, for seasons there are opposite to ours — Tom Zuidema and I had just concluded our second season of work with Earthwatch volunteers at Cuzco, the Inca capital. A drive to the coast seemed more adventurous than a 45-minute flight. And so we made that first trip to Nazca — eight of us in two Volkswagen Beetles loaded on top with suitcases — a three-day roller-coaster ride that averaged about one flat tire every six hours. Cold wind and blowing snow in the mountains at noon gave way two hours later to a balmy 80°F and sunshine in the deep valley of the Apurimac River. Sunset in the chilly air of the high, grass-covered plateau completed the cycle. Detained for three hours by an avalanche and the loss of brakes on one vehicle, we rolled downhill the last ten miles onto the coastal desert, mostly in first gear.

At Nazca we looked at some of Maria Reiche's maps. This remarkable octogenarian emigrated from Germany in 1932 and became a mathematics tutor in Lima. She took over Paul Kosok's work and his astronomy hypothesis, dedicating her life to mapping, clearing, and guarding the lines. Glancing over Maria's drawings, Zuidema, Gary Urton, and I immediately became intrigued by the resemblance between some of her spoke-like patterns of straight lines and the general radial plan of the *ceque* lines of some thousand years later that we had been investigating at Cuzco.

According to Spanish chronicler Juan Polo de Ondegardo's findings, set down by Bernabé Cobo, Cuzco's layout featured four *suyus*, or sectors, divided by roadways leading to remote parts of the Inca Empire. The layout was organized geographically, politically, and socially by 41 imaginary lines, or ceques. These went out from the principal temple, the Temple of the Sun.

Huacas, or sacred places venerated by the people, were arranged along ceques like the knots on a quipu, a string device by which the Inca kept tallies. Each huaca was worshiped at and cared for by members of different economic and kinship classes. In the mid-17th century Cobo described and located each of 328 huacas and stated which kin groups worshiped and sacrificed at each one, even what they sacrificed: "The seventh [huaca of the eighth ceque] was called Sucanca. It was a hill by way of which the water channel from Chinchero comes. On it there were two markers which indicated that when the sun arrived there they had to begin to plant the maize. The sacrifice which was made there was directed to the Sun, asking him to arrive there at the time which would be appropriate for planting, and they sacrificed to him sheep, clothing, and miniature lambs of gold and silver."

While the sun markers have long since vanished, the water channel, the hill, and the town of Chinchero are still there, and Cobo's description has proved accurate, helping us to trace a number of ceques and their huacas by walking the landscape and measuring and mapping the system.

In one river bend where a ceque ends, Cobo tells us, the Inca made sacrifices by dropping objects into the waters. Since the 1950s, Zuidema's studies had indicated that the terminal huacas of many ceques were located in very special places visible on the horizon from Cuzco. Some huacas were part of the vital Inca irrigation system.

Although water was critical in the ceque system, astronomy and the calendar were important, too. Cuzco's ceque lines served multiple purposes. In addition to astronomical alignments and calendrical counting (each huaca may have stood for a day in the agricultural year), ceques often indicated routes of pilgrimage. A 16th-century chronicler speaks of an annual route up the Vilcanota River to higher elevations in the direction of the December solstice sunrise, where the Inca believed their culture had originated. During the Capac Hucha ceremonies, priests led children from tribute villages along these same straight lines to the capital to be sacrificed to the sun god.

Cuzco's ceque system was a highly ordered and basically radial map, a scheme that incorporated important matters connected with the Inca worldview. The calendrical, religious, historical, orientational, ecological, and mythological aspects were interwoven parts of a complex organization that lay on top of the capital city like a huge spoked wheel. Such a scheme surely must have required planning of the highest order, and must have had an earlier and more archaic form. Did the radial Nazca lines — so seemingly ordained by an uncompromising principle of straightness — anticipate Cuzco's ceque system by more than a thousand years?

In the harsh winter confines of the Colgate campus, Urton and I embarked on a program of joint research centered on collecting and analyzing every map and photo of the pampa we could lay our hands on. Piecing visual evidence together, we began to trace a rudimentary pattern of centers and interconnecting radiating lines that spread across the pampa from the Ingenio to the Nazca River, a distance of about ten miles. At least on paper, everything seemed hooked up to something else, and there was much more than Maria Reiche's sketches had indicated.

We needed to know where lines started and where they ended; where they proceeded once they left a center; where the centers of the spoke-like networks of lines were located; and how their locations might be related to a host of other features found on and off the pampa. We needed to return to the desert and set out on foot armed with our maps and photos.

The pampa gave us the answer to the question: Why do most investigators study the lines from the air? Because working conditions on the ground are difficult. We discovered that the most efficient strategy was to rise at 4 a.m., carry hot coffee in a thermos, and have breakfast on the pampa. By sunup we were ready with surveyor's transit in place, and we would spend the morning marking out features in the landscape, our volunteers walking every straight line from start to finish, taking notes and making sketches along the way. As we worked, we could feel the temperature soar from a cool 60°F at dawn to 80° by midmorning, topping 100° by noon. Stinging salt from our perspiration began to seriously affect our vision, and blowing dust rapidly obscured the horizon. By one or two o'clock it was time to leave the hostile pampa, get back to the comfortable environment of the hotel, and work on the data with our calculators.

We found that the lines and line centers are by far the most dominant features on the pampa. Having mapped and measured precise orientations, lengths, and widths of 762 lines emanating from 62 centers, we discovered some interesting patterns. For example, the focal centers bore a remarkable resemblance to one another. Each consisted of a natural hill or low mound, usually topped by a cairn that may have served as an identifying marker.

Standing at the center of one of these mounds and rotating through 360 degrees, you would find yourself confronted with a strange panorama. A dozen or more lines — some wider than a football field, others as narrow as a boot's width — spray outward toward the horizon in all directions, defying topographic relief. Our Earthwatch volunteers and Colgate students were able to follow most of these straight lines several miles to their termination points. About 25 percent appeared to be connected to other centers. Nearly all of the line centers were located either on the last descending hill of a series that protrudes like a finger from the highlands onto the pampa, or on the high dunes that flank the borders of the Ingenio and Nazca Rivers and their tributaries. We found as we walked that many lines opened into large trapezoidal figures. The trapezoids usually had their axes oriented along the watercourses, the narrow ends pointing upstream about two-thirds of the time.

Later we were excited to discover another pattern. The long axes of many trapezoids seemed to correlate with the direction of water flow in another sense. Their wider bases often lay tangent to the banks of the rivers and their tributaries. So if you enter one of these trapezoids by walking along a line, you will invariably find that the upstream direction lies to your right. The intent may have been to impart to the line walker, even when the rivers were dry, a sense of direction relating to the source of water. After all, if you live in the narrow coastal strip of rainless Nazca desert between the high Andes and the Pacific, you need to know where water comes from and how to control it.

Urton's discussions with Nazca locals revealed deep-rooted water cult concepts in contemporary folklore. One old villager told him that in ancient times their ancestors would ascend a prominent mountain named Cerro Blanco — "white hill" — which overlooks the pampa, to pray for rain. They would deposit a vessel of seawater at the summit. If their prayers influenced the god, he would weep gently on the valleys below. Spanish chroniclers referred to Cerro Blanco as part of a pan-Andean scheme of mountain worship dedicated to the bringing of rain.

Our research seemed to add up to at least one certainty about the lines: Their construction was connected in some way with water. The points of arrival and departure and the general direction of movement of this precious liquid onto and across the pampa all strongly correlate to aspects of the Nazca lines and their centers. Were the lines involved in a ritual process related to the calling up of water?

Support for the water hypothesis also appeared in our astronomical studies. Knowing astronomy to have been a part of the ceque system, we looked into whether the Nazca lines pointed to astronomical bodies. We found no correlation with the directions to large land features such as distant mountain peaks and the confluences of major rivers. Nor did we find obvious astronomical correlations. Some lines, however, do intersect the region of the horizon where the sun rises during late October and early November. At that time of year, water begins to run in the rivers and the volume of water increases in the underground canals that honeycomb the pampa's edge. Could solar observations have been used to anticipate water flow?

Another inescapable conclusion about the lines is that they were also pathways. Rarely do we see a line that does not have the remains of one or more footpaths within it, although we cannot be sure of their age. And there are many resemblances between Nazca lines and Andean pre-Columbian roads: sharp kinks and bends, and long straight segments. But why did the ancient people of Nazca walk the lines and line centers? This is something we can never know for sure because the builders left no written record. But our recognition of a certain kind of order on the pampa, both ecological and astronomical, offers a few hints. And Urton's study of documents written after the Spanish conquest bolsters the evidence.

Water allotment was frequently discussed in documents that concerned the partitioning of the valleys by the 16th-century Spanish conquerors. There were careful statements about how the water was to be distributed. They mention different groups of people being allowed to use the irrigation system at different times of the month, based on their location. These documents also revealed that the Andean system of *ayllus* – related groups who shared in communal labor – may have been in use. The ayllus seem to have occupied different river valleys along the coast, and their names can be related to the three social class designations found in the ceque system of Cuzco.

These historical records give clues to the Nazca puzzle. They offer a motive for people to cross the pampa in ancient times, to pass from one river valley to another during assigned periods of work and worship in designated areas. Just as in Cuzco, this activity may have had religious roots. It may have evolved into an elaborate ritual scheme, the parts of which made up the radial network visible on the pampa today. The paths we have traced are capable of taking the walker from one side of the pampa to the other via hundreds of conceivable routes on combinations of narrow lines, wide lines, and trapezoids. We may speculate that, just as huacas on ceque lines were visited and maintained by worshipers designated by kinship class, so too was a Nazca line assigned its walkers and tenders.

Like huacas, the Nazca line centers may have been important places of sacrifice. In the late 1920s, anthropologist Alfred Métraux found that the Cipaya of highland Bolivia used a system of radial pathways leading from far-flung points to a number of centrally located cairns where they deposited offerings to their gods for a propitious planting season. And radial pathways can still be perceived in aerial photos of La Centinela, a pre-Inca pyramid located about 50 miles north of Nazca.

There is enough mystery left in the Nazca lines to keep sleuths occupied for years to come. Why do the trapezoids suddenly widen as you enter them from their skinny, triangular access ways? Why were they built on such a grand scale? The biggest trapezoid we charted measured more than ten football fields in length and two in width. Why trapezoids rather than rectangles? Was it necessary to have blueprints to build such huge figures? What was the origin of the straightness principle that seems to have guided both the Inca and Nazca, two Andean cultures whose centers were a millennium and a mountain range apart?

Where do the animals and plants figure in the scheme? To our surprise, they may not. Mostly isolated in one corner of the pampa, they appear to bear little or no connection to the lines and the geometry. We failed to trace a single line to one of these figures, except in the few instances where a line that had been constructed later ran directly over a figure. If they are effigies like the Uffington Horse or the Serpent Mound, I would not be surprised if these etchings were made to walk upon. Indeed, sculptor Robert Morris sees in the curves of the monkey figure a work to be sensed in a tactile manner by walking on, moving around, or dancing through it.

What we see, feel, and touch there makes more sense when we put ourselves in the place of the artists who sketched and etched on the canvas of the pampa. Our aids to deciphering the puzzle have been part living testimony, part historical record. We may not have decoded all the mysteries of the pampa, but we now know that the etched desert is not a blackboard jungle of confused lines. And I think that its ancient markings were no more intended to be viewed from above than is a Kansas wheat field.

Once we singled out the lines and line centers for study, we found order on the pampa. Evidence points to a ritual scheme involving water, irrigation, and planting. But as we might expect of a culture that did not separate the natural world into compartments — astronomy, geology, biology, meteorology — as we do, elements of astronomy and concepts of a calendar were also present in the pattern. For the moment, our theories offer a rational way to account for the fragile ancient features on the Peruvian desert.

A hummingbird seems to hover on the pampa. Wings of the figure span more than 200 feet. The bird, one of 18 portrayed near Nazca, symbolized fertility in Andean mythology.

· FOLLOWING PAGES: Nazca workers gather dark, desert-varnished rocks to expose the light-colored soil beneath. Others place the rocks to accentuate the edge of their ruler-straight line.

GEORG GERSTER

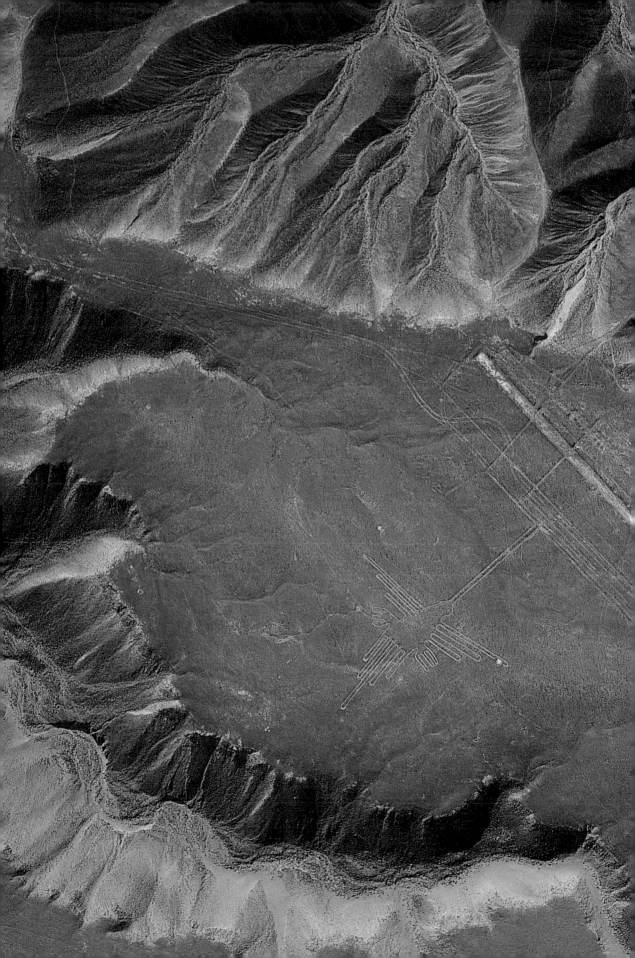

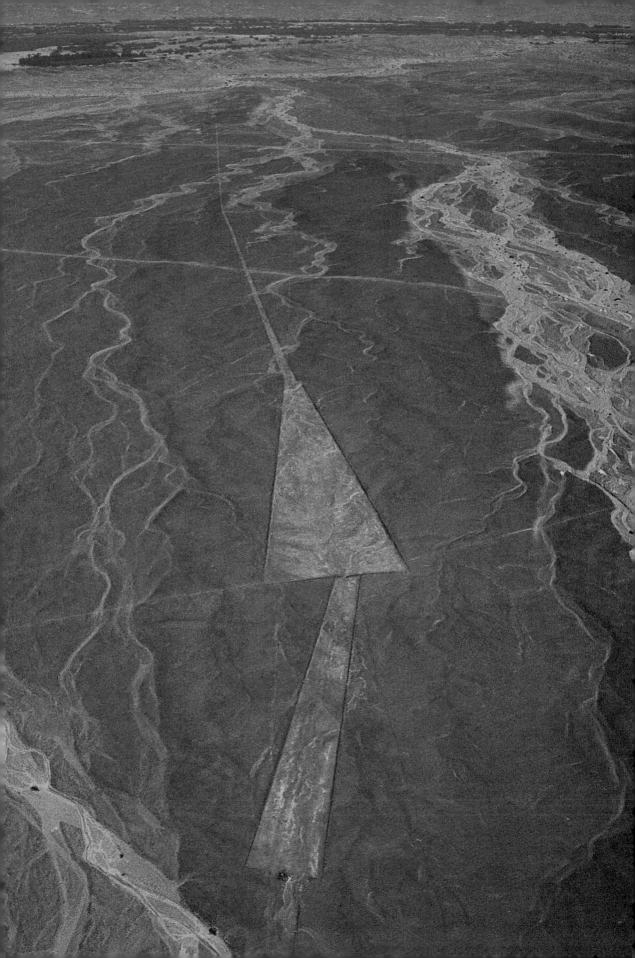

*T*riangles and trapezoids on the Nazca pampa seem to be associated with water. Many of these vast geometric creations, such as those opposite, hug seasonal watercourses, so precious to farmers in this desert environment. At another site (below), a broad band stretches relentlessly true to a center, in foreground, where many lines converge. Scholars surmise that Nazca designs may have set the scene for ceremonial rites and pilgrimages, as well as providing travel routes.

*B*right colors and animal motifs — related in style by scholars to those etched across the desert — mark Nazca crafts. Small birds and flowers form a stitchery fringe (above) that once may have trimmed a funerary shroud or mantle worn by a high-ranking person. Prized ceramic vessels give a glimpse into the world of these long-vanished people. Such pots were often buried by the Nazca. In modern times grave robbers have ravaged many burial sites, hampering the building of an archaeological record. Lizards racing across a slip-painted pot may have symbolized

water, a vital concern for this agricultural society. On the middle jar a Nazca priest, dressed as an important deity, clutches a human trophy head, probably the victim of sacrifice.

A gentler imagery emerges on a third vessel where vividly painted hummingbirds flock. Highly skilled potters, Nazca artists utilized a dozen colors to decorate their wares — more than any other New World culture. These fine, perfectly preserved examples were used as burial offerings and as ritual objects carried in sacred processions.

THE TEXTILE MUSEUM, WASHINGTON, D.C. (TOP); BUCKINGHAM FUND, THE ART INSTITUTE OF CHICAGO (OPPOSITE PAGE); BUCKINGHAM FUND, PHOTOGRAPHED BY ROBERT HASHIMOTO, THE ART INSTITUTE OF CHICAGO (LEFT); MUSEUM, DEPT. OF ARCHAEOLOGY, UNIVERSITY OF CALGARY, PHOTOGRAPHED BY PATRICK CARMICHAEL (ABOVE)

151

*T*orchlight delineates the Nazca drawing known as Needle and Loom. This figure measures about 3,000 feet long. Archaeologists speculate that the Nazca people may have followed these mysterious line designs, etched into the sere pampa landscape, as part of religious observances — perhaps to appeal to the gods for water for good harvests.

FOLLOWING PAGES: *Quipu maker
Nieves Yucra Huatta displays his
handiwork. Quipus, knotted-cord
records of events and inventories,
were used by many Peruvian peoples.*

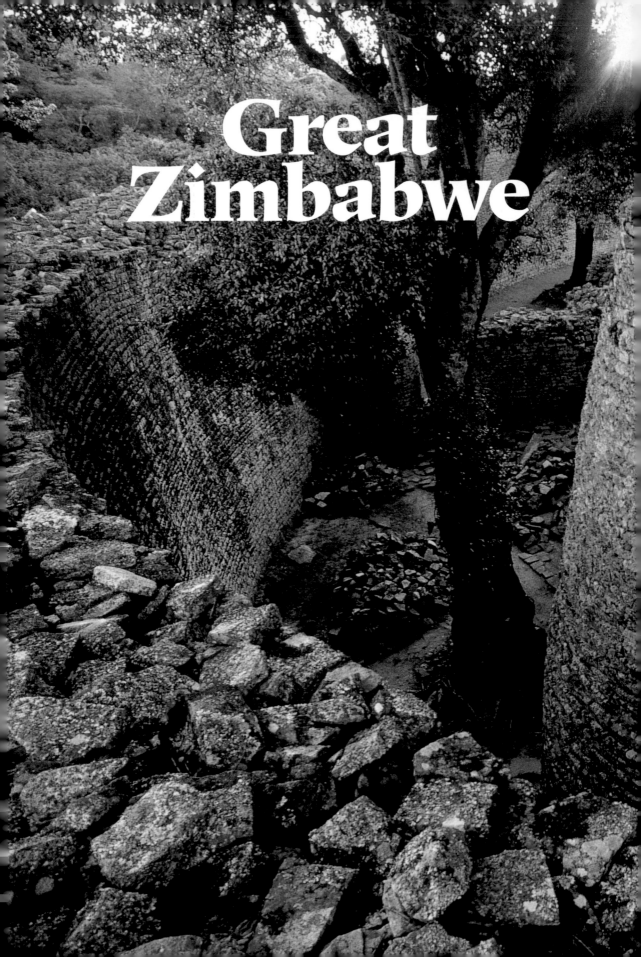

Great Zimbabwe

RICH IN CATTLE AND GOLD

by Brian M. Fagan

The setting sun tinged the African valley in soft pink, casting long shadows from the high stone walls. I stood on a hill in the highest part of the ruins of Great Zimbabwe, looking down on a sprawling maze of enclosures that included the brooding mass of the chief's dwelling place. The silence was profound. A smell of wood smoke drifted up from the nearby farming villages. I shut my eyes and journeyed back across five centuries to the days when Great Zimbabwe was the capital of powerful chiefs of the Shona tribe, rich in cattle and gold. The lords of Zimbabwe once ruled an inland kingdom known to Islamic traders the entire length of the East African coast.

I imagined the excitement when news of an approaching trading party from the coast reached Great Zimbabwe. Iron gongs would ring out as the traders entered the chief's stone-walled enclosure. The chief himself would receive them seated on a low stool and dressed in long cotton robes. He sat surrounded by councillors and relatives wearing strings of gold beads and bright copper wire bracelets. At their throats glistened disks cut from precious white conus shells brought from distant Indian Ocean beaches, ornaments worn only by chiefs and others of great importance. About four centuries later, in 1854, Scottish explorer David Livingstone found that the going price for two conus shells was no less than a slave; for five, a tusk of elephant ivory.

I imagined the traders exchanging gifts with the chief, perhaps presenting him with a wooden box from India inlaid with mother-of-pearl. In return, they accepted a fly whisk made from a hyena tail and decorated with copper wire. Then they laid out strings of brightly colored glass beads, and unwrapped rolls of fine fabric. The bartering would continue for hours—

Soapstone birds of prey, two of several found in the ruins, sit rather than perch and grip with toes, not talons. One such figure has become the symbol of the Zimbabwe nation.

PRECEDING PAGES: The Conical Tower stands in the Great Enclosure at the core of Great Zimbabwe. The grandeur of this ruined city evokes its years as a powerful Shona capital.

beads, porcelain vessels, and fabric traded for gold dust packed in porcupine quills, copper ingots, iron tools, and elephant tusks. Eventually a small caravan of bearers and heavily armed traders would depart for the coast.

In the days that followed, the chief would receive subchiefs and headmen from outlying villages. They would bring gifts of cattle, gold dust, ivory, and copper, and accept exotic imports in return. The chief monopolized all trade with strangers from afar. As a spiritual leader of his people, he was the intermediary between the living and the *vadzimu,* the revered ancestors, the guardians of the land. It was he who could transcend the boundaries between the material and spiritual worlds, ask for rain and protection against disasters such as locust swarms or epidemics, and communicate with the divine forces that governed the fate of his people.

Although, as an archaeologist, I specialized in Africa for many years, I have never excavated at Great Zimbabwe. I have, however, visited the site many times. Invariably it makes a powerful impression on me, as it has on most archaeologists, explorers, and casual visitors. The ruins are the largest and most spectacular of any south of the Sahara. Yet their remoteness in the southeastern highlands keeps them little known outside archaeological circles.

The word "Zimbabwe" comes either from the Shona words *dzimba dza mabwe,* "houses of stone," or, more likely, from *dzimba woye,* "venerated houses," a term still used to describe chiefs' dwellings or graves. Judging from archaeological data, Great Zimbabwe served both these purposes. The Shona applied the word to other chiefs' dwelling places, which were often imposing stone enclosures. But Great Zimbabwe is the largest of all, sprawling across more than a hundred acres, an archaeological site so spectacular and intriguing that it has attracted vigorous controversy for more than a century.

During my first visit in 1960, I gazed up at the low, boulder-strewn Hill Complex that overlooks the green valley. This inconspicuous hill was the most sacred part of Great Zimbabwe. It was here that the chief and his priests performed ancestor rituals and made intercessions for rain. The Hill Complex looks down on the Great Enclosure. I walked in the shadow of the oval-shaped outer wall. More than 800 feet long, it rises more than 32 feet at its highest point. There are three narrow entrances in the wall. I picked my way through a litter of granite blocks and slipped into a cramped passageway between the inner and outer walls.

The stonework dwarfed me as I followed this defile, separated by its inner wall from what had once been the chiefly enclosures within. The passage widened. In front of me stood a conical tower, flat-topped and 30 feet tall, its regular stonework highlighted by the late afternoon sun. Built around a solid masonry core, without stairways or chambers, this remarkable edifice is the most mysterious building at Great Zimbabwe. A clay platform at its base once held stone monoliths, small uprights arranged in careful order. Oral traditions of the Shona tell of large clay bins at other chiefs' enclosures, where tributes of grain were stored. Perhaps the Conical Tower was a symbolic copy of a grain bin and represented the chief's ability to feed his people.

I wended my way through the ruined enclosures that litter the valley floor. Here the chief's many wives may have lived. Then I climbed slowly up a narrow passage that wound between huge boulders to the summit of the Hill Complex. I squeezed through a low, wood-linteled doorway in a granite retaining wall and emerged in the Western Enclosure with its magnificent view of the valley below. The residue of generations of Shona occupation lay underfoot – a remarkable archive of Great Zimbabwe's long history.

I paused to gaze down into the darkening valley, then clambered along twisting pathways into tiny enclosures sheltered among gargantuan weathered boulders. The feeling of isolation, of secrecy, was intense. The Hill Complex had been a sacred place; it was easy to imagine why.

It was here, in 1889, that a German hunter named Willi Posselt saw four carved soapstone birds set into a ruined wall. Amid protest from the local people, he began to hack one bird loose, eventually bartering for two sculptures. Today, a total of eight carved Zimbabwe birds survive. They measure about 12 inches and sit on columns of varying heights. Even ornithologists are baffled by the carvings, which may represent a type of eagle. All have human limbs and four or five toes in front, rather than raptors' talons. The columns bear various symbols, such as chevrons; one has a crocodile crawling upward. We do not know what the animals or V-shaped designs signified.

European visitors found dozens of unadorned stone monoliths about the same size as the enigmatic bird carvings. Some stood along the tops of outer walls; others were grouped on low clay platforms such as those in front of the Conical Tower. Zimbabwean archaeologist Peter Garlake, an expert on the ancient Shona, wonders if the birds and columns represented revered ancestors, for ancestor worship is an important part of Shona religion.

The morning after my arrival dawned gray and damp. The lush grass by the Great Enclosure was slippery underfoot; the boulders on the Hill Complex were mantled in swirling fog. This mist blew through a small valley to the east, from the direction of the Indian Ocean. The landscape is often misty here. Great Zimbabwe is an oasis of green during the long months of winter, when the surrounding countryside lies dry and dusty. This may have been why the Hill Complex was an important center for rain ceremonies and the valley beneath a dwelling place of great chiefs with vast cattle herds.

Towering stone walls, mysterious soapstone birds, boulder-strewn shrines – Great Zimbabwe long intrigued investigator and casual visitor alike. They wondered who built these stupendous walls. Was it powerful African chiefs, or foreign colonists from the Mediterranean world? Stories crediting the ancient Phoenicians have milled around Great Zimbabwe since Europeans first explored southern Africa's shores in the 15th century. Was this the fabled "Land of Ophir" that lay somewhere south or east of Suez? Did King Solomon's ships carry home quantities of gold from mines here?

The Ophir legends began as long ago as 1552. In that year Portuguese historian João de Barros, who never visited Great Zimbabwe, wrote of a land of ancient mines and vast plains in southeast Africa, "in the midst of which there is a square fortress of masonry within and without, built of stones of marvelous size, and there appears to be no mortar joining them." De Barros and his contemporaries assumed that these fabled stone buildings were the work not of illiterate Africans but of a long vanished civilization remembered only in the Scriptures. The legend that Ophir lay in the African bush has persisted ever since.

Such tales brought a young German geologist named Carl Mauch to Great Zimbabwe in 1871. He cut some wood from a door lintel and compared it to his cedar pencil. The sample convinced him that Zimbabwe's doorways were fashioned in part from the famous cedars of Lebanon, and that it was the Queen of Sheba who had built the Great Enclosure!

By the 1890s, when Cecil Rhodes's white colonists flooded north of the Limpopo River into the region that would become Rhodesia, Great Zimbabwe was firmly established in settlers' minds as ancient Ophir. Rhodes himself visited the ruins and proclaimed that "Zimbabye is an old Phoenician residence." More than ten years of sporadic investigations followed, most of them by a journalist named Richard Hall, who was obsessed with Phoenicians. Appointed curator of Great Zimbabwe in 1902, he embarked on a campaign of hasty, unscientific excavation that stripped between three and twelve feet of vital archaeological deposits—along with priceless artifacts—from most of the ruins. He was, he said, removing "the filth and decadence" of African occupation. He believed the Shona were but squatters in a magnificent Phoenician palace dating to as early as 1100 B.C. Hall did such shocking damage to Great Zimbabwe that he was removed from his post. All subsequent excavation has been a matter of piecing together shreds and patches of evidence from the occupation layers his diggers missed.

While Hall wrote about Phoenicians, the British Association for the Advancement of Science sent Egyptologist David Randall-MacIver to Zimbabwe in 1905. Unlike his predecessors, Randall-MacIver was a professional excavator, trained to investigate not only spectacular architecture but small artifacts as well. He worked inside the Great Enclosure at a spot left intact by Hall. He also focused his attention on the tiny glass beads and pieces of medieval Arabian glass discarded by Hall as "rubbish." Far from being useless debris, they were the clues that mattered. Randall-MacIver concluded that Great Zimbabwe had been built not by Phoenicians but by ancestors of the modern Shona some six centuries earlier.

So vicious was the outcry sparked in Rhodesia by Randall-MacIver's findings that no one excavated at Zimbabwe for a quarter century. Randall-MacIver had committed an unpardonable sin in the eyes of the settlers: He had given Africans credit for a tremendous architectural achievement.

By 1929 passions had died down sufficiently for the British Association to commission another round of excavations. This time they chose Englishwoman Gertrude Caton-Thompson, a shrewd and meticulous field archaeologist, who told me she arrived at Great Zimbabwe in an oxcart. "I soon became tired of the Phoenicians," she exclaimed when I took tea with her in Gloucestershire 40 years later. "The settlers thought I was crazy, and I thought their excesses insane." Like Randall-MacIver, she had concentrated on architecture and small artifacts. "There was not a single item that was not of African origin and medieval date," Caton-Thompson said. The so-called mystery of Zimbabwe was solved beyond all reasonable doubt.

In 1958 a team of local investigators—Keith Robinson, Roger Summers, and Anthony Whitty—began excavating at Great Zimbabwe. They had the benefit of the then revolutionary radiocarbon dating method and could date the ruins accurately for the first time. Keith Robinson pieced together the jigsaw puzzle of occupation in the Western Enclosure high atop the Hill

Complex. Thanks to radiocarbon dates, he could prove that Great Zimbabwe had a far longer history than anyone had imagined. Excavations by American archaeologist Tom Huffman in the 1970s firmed up the site's chronology.

The first inhabitants had arrived about A.D. 300 — cattle herders and farmers whose identity is lost to history. Theirs was but a transitory occupation. In fact, they may only have grazed their cattle near where the ruins now stand. For the next 400 years the area was deserted while, elsewhere, Shona groups were building up large cattle herds. By the seventh or eighth century, some of these cattle herding groups had actually settled at Great Zimbabwe. They were farmers with a strong tradition of ancestor worship. As far as we know, they built no stone walls. Zimbabwe soon became a revered shrine and a center for rain ceremonies.

Before 1250, Great Zimbabwe had become one of several major centers on the plateau. The inhabitants enjoyed advantages over their neighbors, one of them being a milder climate than that in the nearby lowlands. To the Shona, cattle were wealth-on-the-hoof, the means whereby chiefs acquired prestige and political power. Cattle flourished in the Zimbabwe region, far from the tsetse-fly-infested lowlands near the coast, where the tsetses carry the parasites that cause sleeping sickness in humans and cattle. Even so, cattle herding was a risky way to acquire wealth because of endemic diseases, droughts, and other hazards. So the chiefs of Zimbabwe turned to the gold and ivory trade, for valuable metal outcrops lay close by and elephants were abundant.

By the tenth century, gold, iron, and ivory were being exported from the southern African interior to a coastal town at Sofala on the Indian Ocean coast. Within two centuries the trade had mushroomed as part of a general expansion of long-distance commerce along the coast. Keith Robinson's excavations date the first appearance of foreign-made glass beads and other exotic objects at Great Zimbabwe to sometime before 1100. But it was not until about 1300 that the main focus of the coastal trade became Zimbabwe. The chief of Great Zimbabwe now acquired a monopoly over local trade, demanding tribute of food, labor, and raw materials from his subjects.

Most of the Great Zimbabwe gold was mined by Shona people living in the area. The miners found surface mineral veins and simply followed them down small shafts hacked out with picks and hoes. Local smiths turned the gold nuggets into small beads or gold dust so that the precious metal could be transported safely and easily.

As Great Zimbabwe grew in political importance, it turned from a large village into a much larger community of packed huts. The commoners' dwellings spread across the valley and the foot of the Hill Complex and up nearby slopes. At the height of its prosperity in the 13th to 15th centuries, Zimbabwe had a circumference of almost three square miles. The elite — the chief himself and the members of his family — lived behind the stone walls of the Great Enclosure. The first structures on the site had been a simple enclosure, a mud hut, and perhaps a storage pit. Soon afterward, the builders — villagers paying tribute to the chief by labor — started work on a stone wall that curves about halfway around the enclosure; then they began to raise the outer walls. The people lavished all their stoneworking expertise on these great walls, taking full advantage of the local granite, which exfoliated naturally in sheets. They would search for outcrops where the rock fractured easily into rectangular blocks that needed little trimming. Modern experiments have shown that setting fires against the rock also causes it to fracture readily, producing dozens of building blocks with little effort.

As many as 18,000 people lived at Zimbabwe during its 14th-century heyday, and it seems certain that the population density eventually exceeded the carrying capacity of the land. Members of the ruling family were already leaving Great Zimbabwe's domains soon after the kingdom came into prominence. They sought better grazing grounds, more farming land, and control of gold and copper outcrops or of trade routes. In some instances, too, they set up competing kingdoms. Wherever they settled, the emerging leaders built miniature copies of the Great Enclosure, albeit often in wood and clay. None of these chiefs controlled territory much more than a hundred miles across — sufficient land to allow the large-scale seasonal grazing of cattle herds.

During the 14th century Great Zimbabwe was a dominant political force on the plateau. A century later the site was abandoned, for reasons still little understood. Centuries of farming and intensive grazing may have exhausted soils that were only moderately fertile in the first place. A mere handful of Shona communities flourished near Great Zimbabwe in the centuries that followed, but the silent ruins were still revered when the first white colonists settled north of the Limpopo River in 1890.

With the fall of Great Zimbabwe, two Shona states dominated the plateau. The first was a little-known kingdom named Butua, or Torwa, centered in the southwest, close to the modern city of Bulawayo. In the north, the kingdom of Mutapa flourished near the Zambezi. By 1500 the Mutapa dynasty ruled over a large tract of gold-rich plateau territory and was trying to control strategic trade routes to the coast. It was this kingdom that Portuguese explorers and missionaries encountered as they arrived on the southeast African coast shortly after Great Zimbabwe's demise. But, five centuries later, it is Great Zimbabwe that has given its name to a vibrant, independent African nation.

Although the ancient Phoenicians are no longer credited with building Great Zimbabwe, many questions still surround this most famous of sub-Saharan archaeological sites. What manner of men were the great chiefs who once dwelled within these walls? What religious and political rites were performed high on the summit of the Hill Complex? And, perhaps most important of all, what ancient beliefs shaped the design of this remarkable place? Future generations of African-born archaeologists will draw on their own cultural experience to offer explanations of a remote and mysterious past.

Dry-stone walls of granite line the narrow, 230-foot-long Parallel Passage. Ancient masons raised the walls of Great Zimbabwe without the aid of mortar, scaffolding, or plumb bob. Between carefully constructed outer faces, each wall is loosely filled with rubble. About a million blocks formed the wall at left, the outer perimeter of the Great Enclosure.

*M*ud-wall houses with thatched roofs (below) reconstruct a village (recently rebuilt) similar to those where most people lived, outside the walled enclosures. A modern musician (opposite) demonstrates Zimbabwe folk instruments: ceremonial drum, leg rattles, and, by his left foot, a mbira — a sort of thumb piano. Panpipes, not traditional here, are probably added for tourists.

PRECEDING PAGES: The chief (seated) observes traders bartering beads, cloth, and Chinese porcelain for gold, ivory, and iron tools — here indicated by hoe blades piled next to some copper ingots. This early Shona capital was an important medieval trading center. On other occasions, this area in front of the Conical Tower was probably used for rituals such as appeals for rain.

WALTER MEAYERS EDWARDS (BOTH)

169

*L*iving rock and layered stones crowd a visitor (below) ascending to the Hill Complex (opposite). This bastion crowns a sheer granite cliff. A privileged class occupied the Western Enclosure (in partial sunlight at top) and conducted rain, fertility, and harvest rites in the Eastern Enclosure (in shadow at bottom). The Hill deftly merges stone walls and buildings with natural boulders. Countless ruins of stone-walled enclosures similar to the Great Enclosure dot the surrounding granite plateau, indicating that Africans, not Europeans, built Great Zimbabwe.

JASON LAURÉ; GEORG GERSTER (OPPOSITE)

NGS PHOTOGRAPHER JAMES L. STANFIELD (UPPER, LOWER, AND FOLLOWING PAGES)

The Great Enclosure's squared, tightly fitted stonework frames a woman wearing a head scarf. The building's sloping outer wall (below) is topped by a double chevron frieze.

FOLLOWING PAGES: Tumbled walls and house mounds trace a former dwelling area near the Great Enclosure. The city's population grew to a peak of 18,000.

Nan Madol

ON THE REEF OF HEAVEN

by Cynthia Russ Ramsay
photographed by James A. Sugar / Black Star

In their days of glory, the rulers of Pohnpei island in Micronesia awed the populace with their power, and the people built a religious and political center made marvelous by its monumental architecture. Basalt boulders weighing as much as 50 tons and thousands of large basalt columns were stacked to create massive structures unrivaled in the palm-fringed realms of the western Pacific. Tombs, ceremonial precincts, and homes of the elite and their attendants dominated the site, which sprawled across some 200 acres just offshore. Landfill of coral rubble enclosed by basalt retaining walls raised a shallow reef area above tide level, creating 92 man-made islets where the enclave known as Nan Madol flourished.

Tunnels made of coral slabs channeled water into pools visited by sacred eels. Storehouses held supplies of coconut oil that anointed the bodies of the nobility in life and upon death. Waterways among the islets carried the traffic of outrigger canoes; laden with yams, taro, and breadfruit, these would pull up to the stone docks, bearing tribute from the main island of Pohnpei to the mighty sovereign, the Saudeleur, in Nan Madol. From their tropical Venice the Saudeleur dynasty governed Pohnpei, a steamy, mountainous island about 13 miles in diameter, lying just north of the Equator. Scholars estimate the population of Nan Madol to have been as many as 1,000, with about 25,000 living in scattered communities on Pohnpei itself.

Much about the Saudeleurs and the construction of Nan Madol remains in doubt. No one knows for sure how the Pohnpeians managed such feats of engineering. How did they raise mammoth rocks as high as 25 feet without beasts of burden or wheeled vehicles? Was it fear or devotion that motivated the swarms of workers who moved countless tons of coral fill and

Heir to the Micronesian seafaring tradition, Candido Wilson polishes a canoe paddle on Pohnpei. Centuries ago islanders created a mighty stone-walled precinct called Nan Madol.

PRECEDING PAGES: Jungle smothers the ruins of Nan Madol, a political and religious center sprawling across 92 man-made islets in a lagoon. Construction began about A.D. 500.

quarried and transported thousands of basalt columns? The baffling ruins keep other secrets: Scholars ponder why Nan Madol was built, why it was located offshore, away from the main island, and why it was abandoned.

By the time the Europeans came upon Nan Madol in the 19th century, they found it deserted and overgrown with vegetation. James F. O'Connell, a shipwrecked seaman who came ashore about 1828 and entertained the Pohnpeians by dancing an Irish jig, was probably the first foreigner to visit the site. In his journal he described the "stupendous ruins" as a place of "deep solitude, not a living thing, except a few birds, being discernible." The native who guided him there "seemed struck dumb with fear" when their canoe landed, and "could not be induced to leave the boat." O'Connell also noted that "fruit grows, ripens, and decays unmolested, as the natives can by no persuasion be induced to gather or touch it."

Other 19th-century visitors also encountered the local reluctance to visit Nan Madol, for the Pohnpeians believed it was haunted by the spirits of their ancient rulers and imbued with the magic powers that had been used to move the huge rocks. Some people are still uneasy about lingering there.

Nevertheless, ceremonies were performed on some islets from time to time. American missionary Luther H. Gulick witnessed a celebration at Nan Madol in 1854 and left an account that provides a glimpse of age-old practices, which for a while survived foreign incursions. Gulick saw a large number of canoes "lashed together so as to form a raft before one of the sacred localities." On board, young men sang to rhythms set by their "small fancifully made paddles." On the 15th day of the feast, a procession of canoes set out from Nan Madol, towing two chiefs in separate boats. "Songs are sung by the little fleet as it passes along, accompanied . . . by the deep monotonous sound" of the conch shell trumpets that echoed sadly across the still waters.

No music or celebration enlivened the labors of Frederick W. Christian, who dug at Nan Madol in 1896. Like the Irishman O'Connell, he found most of the islets shrouded in vegetation, and he wrote of "hewing and hacking . . . tearing away long festoons of creeper and great clumps of weed and fern" before he could begin to dig. Along with numerous skeletal remains, Christian unearthed shell axes, bracelets, pendants, rose pink beads, needles for sewing mat sails, and fishhooks. These artifacts were retrieved from the main burial vault on Nan Douwas, mortuary center of Nan Madol.

An 1840 sketch of Nan Douwas shows a man inside the central vault handing something up to people gathered on top. The caption says the tomb is "supposed to have been of Spanish origin, owing to the discovery of a gold crucifix and silver handled dirk, with some parts of skeletons. . . ." Other finds of silver coins and European artifacts led to a theory in the 19th century that the city was the work of Spanish pirates.

Spanish galleons regularly sailed across the Pacific in the prosperous trade between colonies in Mexico and the Philippines. Today scholars believe the European objects were left on Pohnpei by mariners blown off course on their regular runs between Acapulco and Manila. A local legend remembers the arrival of men with skin so tough they could only be killed by piercing their eyes — presumably a reference to armor.

Some speculations attributed the ruins to Polynesians, Japanese, or residents of the farfetched lost continent of Mu, the Atlantis of the Pacific. European visitors in the 19th century doubted the Pohnpeians built the stone city because, as one trader asserted, "the natives can give no account of it." Another traveler wrote, "The massive ruins of Ponapè are its most remarkable feature, speaking in their weird loneliness of some dead and forgotten race."

In fact, Nan Madol was never forgotten, for it was memorialized in legends passed down for generations. These stories have yielded valuable information about the special function or activities that characterized each islet, and about the Saudeleurs and the priests who resided there.

"This traditional lore would not be shared with passing strangers," said archaeologist J. Stephen Athens, who briefed me in Honolulu, Hawaii, before I continued my journey to Pohnpei, now part of the Federated States of Micronesia. "Islanders hesitate to share such sacred knowledge because they believe if a man reveals everything he knows, he will die. Traditionally, only certain individuals had rights to sacred lore." Like other archaeologists who have worked at Nan Madol, Athens learns what he can from the oral history. He then checks this material against the archaeological record. "But there is no way to document some parts of the legendary history," he added.

Radiocarbon dates from hearth charcoal indicate that people settled at Nan Madol as early as the first century A.D. Around 500 the inhabitants began enlarging sandbars in the shallow lagoon with coral rubble. The splendid megalithic construction, using giant stone "logs" hauled in from the main island (often referred to as the mainland), accelerated between 1100 and 1200 and continued in a massive effort lasting through the 16th century.

Legend attributes the founding of Nan Madol to two brothers—Ohlosihpa and Ohlosohpa—who sailed with their companions from somewhere to the west, "a place downwind." They came with a purpose—to build a place of worship for Nahnisohnsapw, the "Honored Spirit of the Land," bringing with them a "sacred ceremony." After the death of Ohlosihpa, his brother established the dynasty of the Saudeleurs. Stories recall the rulers' absolute power. One despot demanded even the lice from people's heads, decreeing a death sentence for anyone who kept the delicacy for himself. Another monarch required that his subjects collect the dew from taro leaves for his bath.

In that vanished world, tropical growth matted the island's peaks and ridges, and hibiscus bloomed as radiantly red as it does now. The same endless kaleidoscope of clouds brought the torrential downpours that make Pohnpei one of the wettest places on earth. Then, as now, ocean waves crashed against the encircling reef, marking the boundary between azure lagoon and ink blue sea with a wreath of white foam.

Though concrete houses with metal roofs have replaced thatched dwellings, and pickups supplant outrigger canoes, the people continue to live in a highly stratified society whose origins go back to Nan Madol.

"The architecture and artifacts tell us that it was a very status-conscious place," says University of Oregon archaeologist William S. Ayres, who has worked at Nan Madol and at sites on Pohnpei over the past 15 years. "House sizes reflected vast differences in rank. Each level in the social hierarchy rated a house of specific dimensions," he explained. "Shell beads and ornaments were luxury items associated with the upper classes. While these artifacts are not common on the mainland, they are plentiful at Nan Madol, where priests and chiefs resided. Excavations have also identified prestige foods reserved for the elite. These included dog, turtle, and several kinds of large fish, such as parrot fish, which were eaten at feasts."

Such extreme class distinctions no longer exist, but Pohnpei still reserves special privileges for its titled nobility. Even now commoners bow low before high chiefs and pay homage to them with offerings at formal, communal feasts. And when harvesting crops, people present the firstfruits of the land to their district chiefs.

"Protocol at these events quickly reveals who is important," says Pohnpeian archaeologist Rufino Mauricio. "A measure of a man's status is still the number of pigs and the size of the yams he donates to a feast. An 800-pound yam carried on a litter by 10 men makes a very good impression. Of course, a 15-man yam is even better."

Another survivor from bygone days is *sakau,* a slimy narcotic drink essential to every ritual and formal occasion. It is made from pepper plant roots pounded to shreds on a rock with a large, flat surface. Water is poured over the pulp, and the mixture is strained through a wrapping of hibiscus bark strips and wrung into a coconut shell. It is easy to spot the broad sakau stones at Nan Madol, an indication that the rhythmic thwacks that resound through the island today rang through the sacred precinct centuries ago.

While Pohnpeian customs and oral traditions shed some light on the past and evoke the flavor of island life hundreds of years ago, scholars draw much information from the monuments and artifacts. They have dated the stages of islet building. They have mapped the building features on 65 percent of the islets, excavated tools and ornaments, and examined food and skeletal remains. Sometimes archaeology corroborates legend; sometimes there are contradictions. According to tradition, Ohlosihpa and Ohlosohpa made several attempts to establish a settlement, but they abandoned those early efforts because the chosen sites were too exposed to winds, strong currents, and heavy waves. Proof of this story appears in the fragmentary ruins scattered around the main island. On the other hand, archaeologists question the story that the two brothers were invaders or migrants from the west.

"There is no archaeological evidence of a break with the past," says Bill Ayres. "Besides, we don't have to look to another island for the skill and ideas that created Nan Madol. The architecture reflects a gradual expansion of local styles and techniques. Pohnpeians had been using rocks to construct house platforms for centuries, so they had experience in building in stone. Nothing suggests that there were new skills or innovations inspired by foreigners. I believe that a new islandwide political system, not invaders, triggered the sudden massive building program."

The oral history refers to chaotic conditions before the brothers came on the scene. According to *The Book of Luelen,* the first effort to record traditional lore, Pohnpei was divided into numerous feuding clans. "They had no ruler. There were no nobles. . . . There were many among them who would eat their siblings . . . if they had an opportunity." Then, the tale reveals, order was established, the island unified, and the people mobilized in the vast construction project that, with the assistance of magic and the gods, produced the mighty ramparts of Nan Madol.

Like nearly all visitors, I approached Nan Madol from the sea. The ruins are accessible by the rough road that circles the island, but that route requires wading through mangrove swamps and murky canals inhabited by black sea cucumbers and crabs.

Gray wisps of cloud hung over the mountain ridges, but the lagoon was a mirror for dazzling sunlight as I left the state capital, Kolonia, with Emensio Eperiam, Historic Preservation Officer of the Pohnpei State Government. Traveling in a small motorboat, we sped past the fringe of mangrove swamps that holds much of Pohnpei's coastline in a green embrace.

Emensio gives high priority to retrieving Nan Madol from the rampant vegetation. He faces a formidable task in a landscape so lush even telephone poles are said to sprout leaves. Mangrove trees still barricade many of the 92 islets, screening the basalt retaining walls, and jungle brush buries stone house platforms and other traces of the past.

We had been traveling for about 90 minutes when Emensio turned his boat through a break in Nan Madol's seawall into a labyrinth of channels. Immediately we came upon an awesome vista of stone – a cyclopean wall some 200 feet long, 10 feet thick, and 18 to 25 feet high, looming mournfully above the gleaming waters. In the Nan Madol manner it was built of dark gray basalt columns stacked in alternating lengthwise and crosswise rows. The wall was the outer part of a massive, rectangular double enclosure surrounding a central mausoleum. It had unusual upswept corners that came from adding larger stone logs and extra rows to the ends, giving the austere, imposing structure a surprising grace and rough elegance.

We had come to Nan Douwas, the most remarkable site in the ruins. Though more fortress than mausoleum in appearance, it was a place of burial and prayer larger than a football field.

We walked through the main entryway – up the broad, crude steps that led through a gap in the front wall. There were two other entries, so low that you had to crouch to go in. Emensio assumed that, in status-conscious Nan Madol, these were probably designed for use by servants or the lower classes. Just inside was a broad terrace separating the outer wall from the inner one. Coconut palms and slender papaya trees created splashes of shade on the ground. Towering above was a breadfruit tree with a wide canopy of large, glossy leaves that concealed birds calling shrilly from the branches.

We walked slowly along the courtyard between the double walls, passing a small stone burial vault. No paintings or carvings adorned Nan Douwas or any other structures at Nan Madol. No tools had shaped the stones. But the walls possessed a stark, brooding splendor that seemed just the setting for secret and somber rites.

"In ancient times priests would hold ceremonies inside the central vault," said Emensio, as we approached the rectangular crypt where the bones of the Saudeleurs and high priests were interred. Eight basalt columns weighing from four to six tons each made up a flat roof. In the harsh sunlight the empty crypt looked squat and top-heavy, but one could feel its savage power. I could imagine the hush that fell upon the worshipers who prayed there, beseeching their spirits for aid.

We peered into two other small tombs in the outer courtyard. All the tombs are empty now—rifled or excavated in the 19th and 20th centuries. Grave offerings were never sumptuous, for tools were of shell or stone, ornaments were of shell; gold and other metals were unknown. The people had stopped making pottery by about the 12th century, perhaps because coconut shells made good bowls, and pots weren't necessary for baking Pohnpeian-style in an oven made of two layers of hot stones.

In the Pohnpeian language, Nan Douwas means "in the mouth of the high chief," an appropriate name, Emensio explained, because the islet was as concealed from the people as the Saudeleur's own mouth. "Few people were allowed to know what took place within its walls."

Less metaphorical is the name Nan Madol, one translation being "the place of spaces," which refers to the channels among the islets.

The depth of these waterways rises and falls with the tides, which set a timetable for visits to the site. Our outboard required a minimum of 18 inches of water, so we bypassed nearby Kariahn, whose ramparts once guarded the bones of priests. Instead, Emensio maneuvered through the maze of narrow passages that led from the islets of Madol Powe—the upper town, mortuary center, and priests' residence—to Madol Pah—the lower town, ritual center, and administrative headquarters, where the ruler lived.

We moved slowly along dark, silty, sluggish canals, past mangroves propped above the water on exposed, arching roots. The low rock retaining walls that bordered the islets were all but hidden by deep, dank jungle. There was little to see but a lot to wonder about. For if some of the walls were low, the sheer number of these naturally formed basalt logs and the scale of the vast construction were awesome.

I learned from Emensio that there is no doubt about where all the basalt prisms came from. Outcrops of large basalt columns, formed naturally when a kind of molten lava cools slowly, occur at several sites on the main island. But archaeologists can only guess at how those columns, some 3 to 19 feet long and weighing as much as 6 tons, were brought to Nan Madol.

Local people provided some information about quarrying and engineering techniques for German anthropologist Paul Hambruch, who dug at Nan Madol in 1910 and prepared a map of the ruins. Islanders told Hambruch that their ancestors lit great fires, heated the columns, then split them (along natural fissure lines) by pouring cool seawater on them. They transported the building material on rafts, using ropes of tough, strong hibiscus fiber. "The building materials . . . were brought into their present position by means of the inclined surfaces of tree trunks, especially coconut palms, using leverage . . . and the tractive force of Hibiscus ropes," Hambruch noted.

Emensio pointed out that Pohnpeians still routinely move heavy rocks. "Every time any family builds a *nahs*, or feast house, they have to go up into the mountains to get a sakau stone," he said. "Thirty of us, alternating in teams of six, recently transported one with a surface as large as a kitchen table. It was hard labor, but it was fun." I had seen a 1,500-pound yam borne on a litter by 25 men. But what of the boulders weighing between 25 and 50 tons? Wouldn't such rocks sink a raft, especially in the shallow waters around Nan Madol? "We probably will never be sure how such things were moved across miles," said Emensio. "All we know is they were brought here from the mainland."

These marvels are not a mystery to Masao Hadley, a high-ranking chief and historian who has devoted many of his 76 years to compiling lore associated with Nan Madol. Emensio had introduced me to the frail, dignified man in Kolonia, and I recalled his words as we chugged along.

"In those days people knew a prayer called *ahmara* to make heavy things weigh less, and they used this magic to carry rocks on litters and to lift them onto the high walls. Rocks so large they could not be carried were moved through the air into place by the great spiritual power of some of the priests," the chief explained. "Such things don't happen now, but they existed in the days before Christianity came to the island. Even today there are sorcerers who can cause illness and death and others who cure and heal."

We had passed the islet of Dau, where the guards of Nan Madol resided, and Usendau, once inhabited by priests. These were not high-walled islets, and from the boat they presented vistas of green. Had we stepped ashore we would have seen house platforms rising maybe a foot above the surface, with fire pits in the center. An experienced eye would have detected the pattern of holes for posts, which supported walls made of reeds and rafters for the roofs of thatch.

Pahn Kadira was more complex, for it was the residence of the Saudeleur and nearly three times the size of Nan Douwas. Often referred to as the "City of Proclamation," Pahn Kadira had several compounds. Walls up to 16 feet high surrounded the dwelling place of the ruler and his family; lower ones defined an annex for his attendants. Fourteen sakau stones have been found on the islet near the entrance to the main feast house. Untidy with jungle growth, desolate in its emptiness, Pahn Kadira has little left to show how the Saudeleurs led their imperious lives. But the arrogant stone walls still stand, affirming the dynasty's power and authority.

Was Nan Madol a demonstration of political might, an expression of the will to dominate, or was it something more?

University of Hawaii historian David Hanlon believes Nan Madol's offshore location and imposing walls reinforced the distance between the ruler and the ruled. "Distance bred mystery and intimidation," he explains in his book *Upon a Stone Altar,* a history of Pohnpei up to 1890. Clearly the Saudeleurs sought to remain aloof and apart as they "brought order to a contentious land," writes Hanlon, "but it was an order born of domination."

"Nothing would grow in the coral rubble that formed the base of the islets," Hanlon told me. "So the Saudeleurs were faced with the need for tribute in the form of food, as well as the need for labor for the building project that continued throughout their long reign."

"Did the Saudeleurs coerce the populace – or did they try to convince it?" I asked.

"The oral history suggests that the Saudeleurs coerced workers to build their offshore complex of islets," he replied. "They seem to have justified their rule by claims to divine sanction. But I believe the Saudeleurs used force and intimidation, rather than faith or persuasion, to get the Pohnpeians to agree to their demands."

The site itself has a divine association. According to ancient lore, the brothers Ohlosihpa and Ohlosohpa surveyed it from a mountain. When they saw the underwater stairway that leads to the city of the gods, they knew they had found the right location for Nan Madol – on the "Reef of Heaven."

Archaeological discoveries in the past ten years also point to religion as the inspiration for the rise of Nan Madol. "Recent investigations have revealed many more burials than previously suspected and suggest that life at Nan Madol was immersed in ceremony and ritual," says Stephen Athens. He thinks that religion must have been a prime integrating force and that the Saudeleurs probably could not have unified the island without it.

The best known religious center of Nan Madol is the small, strange islet of Idehd, where the saltwater eel, Nan Samwohl, symbol and representative of the Saudeleurs' great god, Nahnisohnsapw, appeared in a sacred pool. "Once a year a ritual was performed here to beseech the god to forgive the people for their sins," said Emensio as we stepped ashore. "A turtle was sacrificed, and its entrails were presented to the eel. If the eel accepted the offering, it meant the god pardoned the people for their transgressions. Then the priests and ruler feasted on the remainder of the turtle."

The first thing we saw was a mound of coral rubble some ten feet high – an accumulation of the stones that had been heated and used to bake turtles for the annual sacrifice. It represented centuries of piety. Unlike other rock, coral crumbles easily; perhaps for this and ritual reasons, the stones were discarded after a single use.

Athens pointed out that the radiocarbon dates for residue from the ovens show that the eel ceremony had begun by around A.D. 1200 – a significant date. It means that ritual activity at Idehd and building with massive basalt columns flourished at about the same time.

Archaeology also tells us that the accumulation of coral debris came to a halt at the same time construction at Nan Madol abruptly ended. This date, about 1600, also coincides with the overthrow of the Saudeleur dynasty and the partition of the island into three separate chiefdoms.

Oral tradition has much to say about how the Saudeleurs were defeated by a man named Isokelekel and his 333 warriors, who rescued the Pohnpeians from the oppressive rule in the last years of the dynasty. Isokelekel assumed power over Nan Madol in the district of Madolenihmw and created the line of Nahnmwarkis, or district chiefs, which commands respect and homage to this day.

With the demise of the Saudeleurs, the impetus to build massive walls was gone. The might and fervor that made it possible to lavish so much energy on Nan Madol had collapsed. But the memory of its greatness lingers on.

Giant prisms of basalt, stacked in Nan Madol's characteristic style, form an enclosure on the islet of Peinkitel. Scholars still marvel at how Pohnpeians moved such huge stones.

FOLLOWING PAGES: Upswept walls 18 to 25 feet tall guard Nan Douwas, where Pohnpeian rulers were buried. Within the walls stand four burial chambers, plundered in the past.

Following age-old custom, guests arrive at a feast bearing a trussed pig (below) as a token of respect. The number of pigs received as gifts confirms the status of the host.

Preparing sakau, *a ritual drink essential to every celebration, a man squeezes the juice from the roots of a pepper plant into a coconut-shell cup. The roots, wrapped in wet*

strips of hibiscus bark, were first pounded to a pulp on large, flat stones selected for their resonance. Archaeologists have found such sakau stones at Nan Madol.

Below the landmark Sokehs Rock (center rear), members of an outrigger canoe club practice for an upcoming race that calls forth ancestral skills.

FOLLOWING PAGES: Inside the impressive walls of Nan Douwas, basalt logs litter the gallery around the main burial chamber. When

vegetation roots in spaces between the stones, it pries them apart, toppling columns quarried on the main island and transported here.

Notes on Contributors

ANTHONY F. AVENI earned his Ph.D. at the University of Arizona and teaches at Colgate University. He helped found and develop the field of archaeoastronomy, concentrating his studies on the astronomy of the ancient peoples of the Americas.

English-born BRIAN M. FAGAN holds a Ph.D. from Cambridge University and teaches anthropology at UCLA, Santa Barbara. His many books include the Society's *Adventure of Archaeology*.

Artist H. TOM HALL has contributed many paintings to Society books, including 15 archaeological recreations for *America's Ancient Cities*. A book illustrator for 34 years, he specializes in historical subjects.

ANN NOTTINGHAM KELSALL has taught English language and American culture at Xi'an Jiaotong University. On staff since 1983, she wrote about ancient Chinese architecture in *Builders of the Ancient World*.

Staff writer TOM MELHAM first visited the Bighorn Medicine Wheel in 1974 on a Magazine assignment. This time he found the site "still magnetic and mysterious." He wrote the chapter on Egypt's pyramids in *Mysteries of the Ancient World*.

CYNTHIA RUSS RAMSAY, a staff writer, has often written about archaeology. Her contributions include chapters in the Society's *Splendors of the Past* and *Mysteries of the Ancient World*.

Writer and editor GENE S. STUART wrote *The Mighty Aztecs* and *America's Ancient Cities* and co-authored *The Mysterious Maya* with her archaeologist husband, George. They are currently collaborating on a new Society book about the Maya.

GEORGE E. STUART, staff archaeologist, has a Ph.D. from UNC, Chapel Hill. Since joining the staff in 1960, he has written many articles for the Magazine and has contributed to several Society books.

Photographer JAMES A. SUGAR, associated with the Black Star agency, has free-lanced for the Society since 1969. He found Nan Madol structures "more incredible than I could possibly have imagined."

Archaeologist JO ANNE VAN TILBURG earned her Ph.D. at UCLA, where she now teaches. Her extensive fieldwork on Easter Island inspired her forthcoming book, *Easter Island: Spirit in the Stone*.

Acknowledgments

The Book Division is extremely grateful for the assistance given by the individuals named or quoted in the text and by those cited here: Greg Anderson, Cristián Arévalo Pakarati, Patti and Bob Arthur, Gene Ashby, William J. Dewey, Richard G. Forbis, Alice Kehoe, Miquel Marquez, George T. Mvenge, Michael Nylan, Anne Paul, Nancy Shatzman Steinhardt (translation, page 53), David S. Stuart, Richard F. Townsend, John W. Verano.

Additional Reading

The reader may wish to consult the *National Geographic Index* for articles and books. In addition, we found the following books of particular interest:

Prologue: Rodney Castleden, *The Knossos Labyrinth;* J. P. LePre, *The Egyptian Pyramids;* Stephen Williams, *Fantastic Archaeology.*

Palenque: William M. Ferguson and Arthur H. Rohn, *Mesoamerica's Ancient Cities;* Merle Greene Robertson, *The Sculpture of Palenque: Volume I;* Jeremy A. Sabloff, *The Cities of Ancient Mexico.*

Mount Li: Wen Fong, ed., *The Great Bronze Age of China;* Qian Hao, Chen Heyi, and Ru Suichu, *Out of China's Earth;* Arthur Waldron, *The Great Wall of China.*

Easter Island: Paul Bahn and John Flenley, *Easter Island Earth Island;* Alfred Métraux, *Ethnology of Easter Island;* Katherine Routledge, *The Mystery of Easter Island.*

Stonehenge: Christopher Chippindale, *Stonehenge Complete;* Julian Richards, *English Heritage Book of Stonehenge.*

Medicine Wheels: Ake Hultkrantz, *Belief and Worship in Native North America;* Ray A. Williamson, *Living the Sky.*

Nazca Lines: Anthony F. Aveni, ed., *The Lines of Nazca;* Marilyn Bridges and John Hyslop, *Planet Peru;* Evan Hadingham, *Lines to the Mountain Gods.*

Great Zimbabwe: Graham Connah, *African Civilizations;* Peter S. Garlake, *Great Zimbabwe;* Martin Hall, *Farmers, Kings, and Traders.*

Nan Madol: Gene Ashby, *Pohnpei, An Island Argosy;* David Hanlon, *Upon A Stone Altar;* William N. Morgan, *Prehistoric Architecture in Micronesia.*

Index

Boldface indicates illustrations.

Library of Congress ℂℙ Data
Mysteries of mankind : Earth's unexplained landmarks / prepared by
  the Book Division, National Geographic Society.
      p. cm.
    Includes index.
    ISBN 0-87044-864-1
    1. Megalithic monuments. 2. Earthworks (Archaeology) 3. Sacred
  space. I. National Geographic Society (U.S.). Book Division.
  GN790.M97 1992
  930 – dc20   92-22242
                                                             ℂℙ

Composition for this book by the Typographic section of National Geographic Production Services, Pre-Press Division. Set in Hiroshige Book.
Printed and bound by R. R. Donnelley & Sons, Willard, Ohio. Color sep-
arations by Graphic Art Service, Inc., Nashville, Tenn.; Lanman Pro-
gressive Co., Washington, D.C.; Lincoln Graphics, Inc., Cherry Hill,
N.J.; NEC, Inc., Nashville, Tenn.; and Phototype Color Graphics, Penn-
sauken, N.J. Dust jacket printed by Federated Lithographers-Printers,
Inc., Providence, R.I.